KILLING DEFENCE AT BRIDGE

Killing Defence at Bridge is one of the great all-time classics of bridge. It carries the mark of genius and was the first of a series of major books written by Hugh Kelsey, who became internationally recognised as a leading authority on the analysis of bridge. He coupled this incisive thinking with a brilliant skill with words – hardly surprising as he had hitherto written only novels – and made the most complex techniques in bridge sound simple and easy to grasp.

Ron Klinger has written a splendid new foreword to this wonderful book which is as relevant today as when it was first published.

KILLING DEFENCE AT BRIDGE

Hugh Kelsey

CASSELL&CO
IN ASSOCIATION WITH
PETER CRAWLEY

First published in 1966 by Faber & Faber Ltd
New edition first published 1992
in association with Peter Crawley
by Victor Gollancz
This edition with new Foreword first published 1997
Fourth impression 2005
in association with Peter Crawley
by Cassell
Wellington House, 125 Strand, London WC2R 0BB
an imprint of the Orion Publishing Group

The right of Hugh Kelsey to be identified as author of this book has been asserted
by him in accordance with the Copyright, Designs and Patents Act 1988

A catalogue record for this book is available from the British Library

ISBN 0-304-35777-4

Printed and bound in Great Britain by
Mackays of Chatham, Chatham, Kent

www.orionbooks.co.uk

This book is dedicated to the members of Perth Bridge Club in appreciation of many happy games there

Contents

Foreword

Shortly after 1966, contracts which had hitherto been routinely successful were being regularly defeated. Players who were wont to drop a trick here and a trick there had suddenly become niggardly. No doubt many declarers rued the appearance of *Killing Defence at Bridge* which was to blame for their reduced rate of success in dummy play.

It is but rarely that a book appears which can change our perception, out whole approach to the play of the cards. *Killing Defence at Bridge* was such a watershed. It brought light where there was darkness and taught countless players the right way to think about defending. There can scarcely be an expert player in the world who is not indebted in some degree to this exceptional work of analysis and clarification.

Hugh Kelsey was one of *the* great bridge writers. He wrote many outstanding books but to me, his best has always been and will be *Killing Defence*. I was lucky enough to come across it at the start of my bridge career and many early successes can be directly attributed to the lessons it imparted. The counting, the signalling, the inferences – it was such an eye-opener and I devoured it all. Then I read and re-read it several times each year. Even now it sits on my nearest bookshelf where I often dip into it, for the pleasure in reading and solving its problems has scarcely diminished.

Killing Defence has become a deserved classic and it still retains the Kelsey spark of genius. If you are only just starting this wonderful work, I am thoroughly envious. You are about to embark on a voyage of discovery, a voyage that will give you hours and hours of enjoyment and reward. Happy sailing.

Ron Klinger, 1997

Introduction

It is generally agreed that defence is the most difficult part of the game of bridge. Although after the opening lead both sides can see twenty six of the fifty-two cards, the declarer has a two fold advantage. Firstly he has full knowledge of the strength and disposition of his forces, and secondly he is in sole command of the play. The defenders, on the other hand, labour under a double handicap. Not knowing their exact strength they have to compensate by developing their powers of counting and deduction. And, since the very fact that there are two defenders makes a defensive error twice as likely, a high degree of partnership co-operation is required.

The average defender operates in a fog of uncertainty. He makes elementary mistakes because his mind has not been trained to think along the proper lines. His blunders are mainly due to faulty logic, failure to count and failure to draw simple inferences. Experts also slip up quite frequently in defence, but in their case the cause is usually a lapse in concentration. A high level of sustained vigilance is needed in order to defend without error.

This book is not for the beginner, for I have assumed a knowledge of technique that the beginner will not possess. It is written for the great mass of players from average up to near-expert standard, in the hope that a short course in logical thinking may help them to defeat more contracts than they do at present.

1 • Counting

If you think this a dull subject to start with, you had better trot straight back to the bookseller and see if he will refund your money. For the same theme runs through every page of this book. Counting is a subject that the serious student cannot afford to neglect. It is impossible to produce consistently tight defence unless both defenders make a conscious effort to count the hand.

The chances are that if you asked an average seven-year-old to add five and four and one and subtract the total from thirteen he would come up with the right answer. Why is it, then, that so many intelligent adults produce the wrong one at the card table? Mostly it is a matter of mental laziness. You know very well that you ought to count, but when partner shows out on the second

15

round of trumps you merely register hazily that declarer must have quite a lot without making the effort to work out just how many.

That is understandable, for although the arithmetic is simple the effort required is very real. It is an extra demand on your concentration at a time when you already have plenty on your mind. You may be worried because your opening lead has turned out poorly. You are busy studying the dummy, evaluating its dangers and its weaknesses, noting that your king of clubs is well placed and wondering if partner could have the ace of diamonds. You are trying to make up your mind what to do if declarer should lead the knave of hearts through your queen. You are mustering your technical resources, culled from past experience of similar hands. You are watching every card played by your partner and the declarer and trying to read some significance into them, and the extra effort of trying to count the declarer's hand seems hardly worth while.

My job is to try and convince you that it is very much worth while. If you get your priorities right and put counting first you will find that many of your other problems will resolve themselves.

Counting may take one of several different forms. What is usually called counting the hand means counting declarer's and your partner's shape; in other words, working out the distribution of each suit in the unseen hands. An exact count will not often be possible until fairly late in the play of the hand and it may be necessary for the defenders to take action earlier, so they often have to rely on an inferential count. By drawing inferences from the bidding, from the declarer's line of play and from their partners' leads and signals, they build up a picture of the unseen hands on which they base their defence. Sometimes the only available count is a hypothetical one. When the only danger (or the only hope) lies in a certain distribution, the defenders must assume that distribution to exist and base their whole defence on the assumption.

Another profitable form of counting that is sadly neglected by many players is the counting of declarer's tricks. When it is clear that declarer will make enough tricks for his contract as soon as he gets in, the defenders must hasten to cash their quick winners. Conversely, when declarer appears to be a couple of tricks short that is the time to play a passive defence and give him no assistance whatever. At times it will be necessary to count only the defensive tricks. The question: 'Where is the setting trick to come from?' will often admit of only one logical answer.

Keeping a careful count of declarer's points is a valuable habit that will often show the way to the best line of defence. The bidding sequence usually gives some indication of declarer's values. By relating his bidding to the number of points declarer has shown up with it will frequently be possible to infer that he must have (or cannot have) a particular honour card.

These different forms of counting are not, needless to say, mutually exclusive. You may have to combine the counting of shape, tricks and points in the one hand. In most hands it is a happy blend of counting and logical deduction that is required in order to avoid error and find the killing defence.

No attempt has been made in this chapter, or indeed throughout the larger part of the book, to classify the hands on a technical basis. The emphasis is not on defensive technique but on card reading. Any technique you may absorb from these pages, therefore, will be incidental (my partners might prefer to say accidental).

Here is a simple hand to start with.

You lead the ace of diamonds against South's four heart contract, your partner playing the four and declarer the three. How should you continue?

Those who wish to treat this book as a course of study rather than a light entertainment should pause at this point in each problem before going on to read the solution. The road to improvement lies in making a real effort to work out the answer for yourself.

Were you listening to the bidding? Then you will know that South has at least ten cards in the major suits, and therefore not more than three in the minors. If he has two losing clubs he will be able to get one of them away on the king of diamonds as soon as he gets in, so there is no time to waste. You must lead the three of clubs at once in order to be sure of taking any club tricks that are due to you. There is no need to worry about the possibility of South having ace and another club, for in that case his small club will disappear on the king of diamonds anyway. Thus the club switch cannot lose a trick, and it may be essential in order to beat the contract.

The hidden hands:

♠ Q 9 4
♡ A 9 6
◇ 3
♣ K Q J 8 7 2

S	N		♠ 7 5 2
1 ♡	2 ♣		♡ K 8
2 NT	3 ♡		◇ Q 9 6 5
4 ♡	—		♣ A 9 5 4

Your partner leads the three of clubs against South's four heart contract. The two is played from dummy and South plays the ten under your ace. How should you continue?

This is a simple matter of counting your own tricks and getting the timing right. Partner's three of clubs is an obvious singleton so you can give him a ruff, and the king of hearts will be the third defensive trick. Where is the setting trick to come from? Either partner must have an ace, in which case the order in which you take your tricks is immaterial, or he will have to have the king of spades. In the latter event you must play the defence with care. Suppose you lead a club and give partner his ruff immediately. He will be unable to attack spades from his side so he will lead, say, a trump. Your king will be allowed to win, and when you lead a spade declarer will go up with his ace, draw trumps ending in dummy and discard his spade losers on the clubs.

To be sure of making all the tricks available to the defence, you must lead a spade at trick two. There is no need to hurry to give your partner his ruff. On the bidding he is marked with three trumps and the ruff can safely be postponed.

The unseen hands:

♠ K 10 6 3
♡ 5 4 2
◇ J 10 8 7 4
♣ 3

♠ A J 8
♡ Q J 10 7 3
◇ A K 2
♣ 10 6

Three no trumps is, of course, a superior contract.

♠ 9 6
♡ K J
◇ A J 4
♣ Q J 10 9 7 2

♠ Q J 10 8 5 3
♡ 7
◇ Q 10 7
♣ A 8 4

N	E	S	W
1♣	—	1♡	1♠
2♣	—	3 NT	All pass

Against South's three no trump contract you lead the queen of spades, East following with the four and South with the two. How do you continue?

First, what is the spade situation? Your partner must have either a singleton or a doubleton, and declarer has held up his ace and king. Then there can be no point in continuing spades since when your partner gets in he will be unable to return the suit. What inference can be drawn from the fact that declarer has held up in spades? Clearly your partner must have a sure entry, either the ace of hearts or the king of clubs. With both these cards declarer would not have ducked the first spade. He would have won immediately and knocked out your ace of clubs and claimed at least ten tricks. One spade trick in the bag, the ace of clubs and your partner's entry adds up to three tricks for the defence, and you need to develop two more. A heart switch cannot be right, for in the unlikely event that your partner has A Q 10 you will have a chance to lead hearts later. But if declarer's weakness is in diamonds it may be essential for you to attack the suit now. Your partner's diamonds will have to be K 8 x or better, and you must lead the ten to trap dummy's knave.

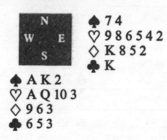

♠ 7 4
♡ 9 8 6 5 4 2
◇ K 8 5 2
♣ K

♠ A K 2
♡ A Q 10 3
◇ 9 6 3
♣ 6 5 3

When a count of the hand has shown you a sure way of setting a contract, you must not allow cupidity to deflect you into a less certain path.

```
            ♠ A Q 7 2
            ♡ 9 8 6 2
            ◇ A K 9 4
            ♣ K

♠ 5                          S        N
♡ K 10 5 4                   1 ♠      3 ◇
◇ J 3                        3 ♠      4 ♠
♣ A J 7 6 4 2                5 ♡      6 ♣
```

You make a dubious trump lead against South's spade slam. Declarer wins and continues with a second round of trumps to which your partner follows. Three rounds of diamonds are won by the ace, queen and king, and the nine of diamonds is covered by your partner's ten and ruffed by declarer, who now exits with the queen of clubs. On winning with the ace what do you lead?

This is a fairly easy hand to count. Declarer appears to have a 6-3-3-1 distribution and he is certainly going down in his contract. In fact if partner has queen and another heart, a heart lead from you will ensure a two-trick defeat. But wait a minute. Are you quite sure declarer's queen of clubs was a singleton? With queen and another it would cost him nothing to play the queen on the chance of inducing a miscount. Even if declarer has no more clubs a club lead cannot give him the slam, and that is your only proper return.

```
                          ♠ 9 3
                          ♡ J 7 3
                          ◇ 10 8 5 2
                          ♣ 10 9 8 3

            ♠ K J 10 8 6 4
            ♡ A Q
            ◇ Q 7 6
            ♣ Q 5
```

Sometimes, as in the next deal, a simple count will shed such a brilliant light that all four hands are visible at trick one.

```
              ♠ A 8 7 4
              ♡ A 6 5
              ◇ Q J 10 2
              ♣ J 2
    S      N                    ♠ K 10 2
    1 ♡    1 ♠                  ♡ K 8 7 4 2
    1 NT¹  3 ♡                  ◇ 7
    3 NT   —                    ♣ K 10 9 4
```

Your partner leads the three of clubs and the two is played from dummy. How do you plan the defence?

If West had a five-card suit he would probably have led it, so his distribution is likely to be 4-1-4-4. He would not have led his lowest club from four headed by the eight, so he will have an honour. Could it be the queen? Only if declarer is a very poor player, for with three clubs to the ace in his hand his proper play would be the knave from dummy. Partner has the ace of clubs then, and it is time to count points. Add partner's ace to the twenty-one points you can see and it leaves only fifteen for declarer. He must have every outstanding face-card.

You now know everything, so we may as well put down the other two hands and treat this as a double dummy problem.

```
    ♠ 9 6 5 3
    ♡ 10
    ◇ 8 6 4 3
    ♣ A 7 6 3

              ♠ Q J
              ♡ Q J 9 3
              ◇ A K 9 5
              ♣ Q 8 5
```

Clearly you must not duck the first club, or declarer will make nine tricks before you can make five. Spades cannot be attacked from your hand so, after winning the king of clubs, you must return the four of clubs to your partner's ace. Your partner will also be counting and he will realize that a spade switch is required at trick three. If your king of spades is allowed to win you will, of course, switch back to clubs.

¹ The 1 NT rebid shows 15–16 points.

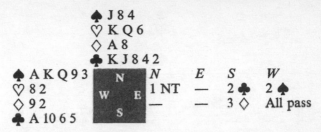

♠ J 8 4
♡ K Q 6
◇ A 8
♣ K J 8 4 2

♠ A K Q 9 3
♡ 8 2
◇ 9 2
♣ A 10 6 5

N	E	S	W
1 NT	—	2 ♣	2 ♠
—	—	3 ◇	All pass

Against South's contract of three diamonds you start off with three rounds of spades, declarer ruffing the third round. The queen of diamonds is led and run to your partner's king. East returns the nine of clubs and South plays the three. How do you defend?

If your partner's nine of clubs is a singleton you can defeat the contract by giving him a club ruff. But first see if you can count the hand. Declarer had two spades and presumably five diamonds (if he had only four he is going down anyway). He must have four hearts or he would not have inquired for majors, therefore he cannot have more than two clubs. Since a club ruff for partner is no longer a possibility, your best chance is to take your ace of clubs and continue with a fourth round of spades. Declarer has surely no losers left in the side suits, so the ruff and discard cannot help him. On the contrary it is likely to embarrass him considerably, and if your partner's remaining diamonds are as good as 7 6 3 it will defeat the contract for certain.

♠ 10 6 5
♡ 9 7 5 3
◇ K 7 6 5
♣ 9 7

♠ 7 2
♡ A J 10 4
◇ Q J 10 4 3
♣ Q 3

You will be doing well if you score full marks on the next problem because, for the first time, you have to rely on a hypothetical count.

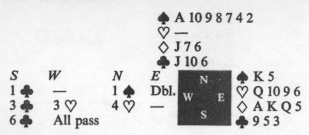

♠ A 10 9 8 7 4 2
♡ —
◊ J 7 6
♣ J 10 6

S	W	N	E		♠ K 5
1 ♣	—	1 ♠	Dbl.		♡ Q 10 9 6
3 ♣	3 ♡	4 ♡	—		◊ A K Q 5
6 ♣	All pass				♣ 9 5 3

Your partner leads the three of diamonds and the six is played
from dummy. How do you plan the defence?

What do you know? Firstly, that South has one diamond (on
the bidding he can hardly have two). Secondly, that he very likely
has all seven outstanding trumps. But what is his spade holding?
That is the crucial matter. If declarer has more than one spade he
will be unable to avoid a spade loser, but if he has a singleton he
will be able to set up dummy's spade suit for all the discards he
needs. Since there is danger only if declarer's shape is 1-4-1-7, you
must defend on the assumption that it is so.

Declarer will be unable to make use of dummy's spades if you
can force him to ruff a heart on the table at trick two. Partner
will have to have the heart ace to give you a chance, but then
declarer might have K J in hearts, in which case, if he makes
the right guess, his knave will force partner's ace and he will
come to twelve tricks by way of a cross-ruff. He might guess
wrong, however, if he thought your partner had led from the
king of diamonds. Your best chance is to win the first trick with
the diamond ace and lead the ten of hearts. Declarer will be suspicious, but he may suspect you of the wrong subterfuge and go up
with the king of hearts.

♠ Q 6 3
♡ A 8 5 4 3
◊ 10 8 4 3 2
♣ —

♠ J
♡ K J 7 2
◊ 9
♣ A K Q 8 7 4 2

♠ J 6 5
♡ 6 2
◇ A J 10 9 3
♣ 10 6 4

S	N
2 NT	3 NT

♠ K 8 2
♡ J 8 3
◇ Q 7 5
♣ K J 9 3

Your partner leads the ten of hearts, on which you play the eight and declarer the seven. West continues with the five of hearts and your knave is captured by declarer's ace. South leads the two of diamonds, your partner plays the four and dummy the nine. How do you plan the defence?

Partner clearly led from a five-card heart suit headed by Q 10 9 (although if declarer had won the second heart with the king you could not have been sure of this). If partner had only two diamonds he might have echoed to show his distribution. Even if yours is the kind of partner who has never heard of an echo you should still duck this trick, for if declarer has three diamonds to the king his contract is unbeatable anyway. A count of the points will show you why. Giving declarer the ace and king of hearts and the king of diamonds, he must also have both black aces and at least one of the black queens for his bid of two no trumps. Two heart tricks, four diamonds and three tricks in the black suits adds up to nine, so the only hope for the defence is that declarer's diamond holding is K 2.

♠ Q 9 3
♡ Q 10 9 5 4
◇ 8 6 4
♣ 8 5

♠ A 10 7 4
♡ A K 7
◇ K 2
♣ A Q 7 2

Even after you duck the diamond declarer may still get home if he makes a series of inspired guesses, but that does not affect the lesson of the hand.

```
              ♠ J 5
              ♡ K 8 7 5 2
              ◇ Q J 10 9
              ♣ A 2
♠ K 8 7                        S        N
♡ Q 9 3        N               1 ◇      1 ♡
◇ 7 4       W     E            1 ♠      3 ◇
♣ 10 9 8 7 5   S               3 NT     —
```

Your lead of the ten of clubs is won by partner's king, and he returns the three of clubs, South following with the four and six. Declarer runs three rounds of diamonds, your partner's king falling to the ace on the third round while you discard a club. Now comes the six of spades from the declarer's hand. How do you defend?

What was partner's original club holding? With K Q J 3 or K Q 3 he would not have played the king at trick one, and with K J 3 he would have returned the knave, not the three. So you are forced to the conclusion that partner had only K 3 in clubs and declarer Q J 6 4. But declarer bid diamonds and then spades, therefore he must have a singleton heart. Now count his tricks. He has four in diamonds and three in clubs. The ace of hearts, along with dummy's king, would give him nine tricks, so you ignore that possibility. And if his singleton heart is anything but the ace you can set the contract for sure by pouncing on this trick with your king of spades and leading the queen of hearts. It would be fatal to play low to this trick, for South certainly has the ace and queen of spades (count his points) and the knave of spades would be his ninth trick.

```
                              ♠ 10 4 3 2
              N     E         ♡ A 10 6 4
           W     E            ◇ K 3 2
              S               ♣ K 3
♠ A Q 9 6
♡ J
◇ A 8 6 5
♣ Q J 6 4
```

♠ 10 8
♡ A 3
◇ K Q 7 2
♣ Q 10 9 6 4

```
S        N                    ♠ 7 3
1 ♠      2 ♣                  ♡ K 7 6 2
2 ♡      2 NT                 ◇ A J 8 5
4 ♡      4 ♠                  ♣ K 8 7
```

Your partner leads the ten of diamonds against South's four-spade contract and your ace captures dummy's queen. How do you plan the defence?

This problem is very similar to the first one. Again you know from the bidding that South has not more than three cards in the minor suits so you must go for the clubs. If declarer has the ace of clubs your partner will need to have two trump tricks to defeat the contract and you can forget about that possibility. How should you tackle the clubs? This time it is not good enough to lead a small club. The king is the proper card to play whatever declarer's holding may be. If South has a doubleton diamond and a singleton club it is vital that you lead the king of clubs first so that declarer will have to ruff in front of your partner's ace. That will cause him to lose control if he has only five trumps. And should declarer have a singleton diamond and two small clubs you want your partner to be on lead after the second club trick in order that he may knock out dummy's heart ace before it can be used as an entry for the minor suit winners.

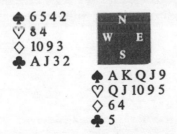

♠ 6 5 4 2
♡ 8 4
◇ 10 9 3
♣ A J 3 2

♠ A K Q J 9
♡ Q J 10 9 5
◇ 6 4
♣ 5

2 • Beating the Drum

While not forgetting the main theme of counting, we shall take a look, in this chapter, at some of the standard signals and other means of communication (legal ones, of course) that the defenders have at their disposal.

All readers who have not dropped out by now will be familiar with the Rule of Eleven. The conventional lead of the fourth highest card from a long suit is the simplest and the most effective single aid to counting and good defence that has been devised. Yet many players do not appreciate the full implications of this convention and thus fail to derive the maximum benefit from it.

The advantage usually claimed for the Rule of Eleven is that it enables the defenders to run a suit without interruption in a situation such as this.

K 5 3

Q 10 8 7 4   A J 9 2

6

When West leads the seven of spades again a no trump contract, East will subtract seven from eleven and, if he is in form, arrive at the answer of four. Since he can see all four cards higher than the seven in his own and dummy's hand, he knows it is safe to play his two and allow his partner to retain the lead.

All very well, but the situation occurs so seldom that the Rule of Eleven would hardly be worth the effort of remembering if its usefulness were confined to that. Here are a few hands to illustrate some other ways in which the Rule can be applied.

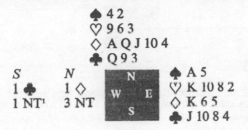

```
                ♠ 4 2
                ♡ 9 6 3
                ◇ A Q J 10 4
                ♣ Q 9 3

S       N                       ♠ A 5
1♣      1◇                      ♡ K 10 8 2
1 NT¹   3 NT                    ◇ K 6 5
                                ♣ J 10 8 4
```

West leads the six of spades to your ace, declarer playing the seven. How do you continue?

The Rule of Eleven tells you that declarer started with four spades higher than the six. He surely has a spade stopper then, for with any sort of sequence partner would have led an honour. You know the next step—count declarer's tricks. He will have three club tricks, he can develop four diamonds, so two tricks in the majors would see him home. It would clearly be fatal to continue spades; you must switch to hearts while there is still time. Partner will have to have the queen, and you should lead the ten to trap declarer's knave.

```
♠ K 10 8 6 3
♡ Q 5 4
◇ 8 7 2
♣ 6 2

                ♠ Q J 9 7
                ♡ A J 7
                ◇ 9 3
                ♣ A K 7 5
```

The Rule of Eleven can be applied from either side of the table, not only on the opening lead but also when partner returns your suit.

___

¹ 15–16 points.

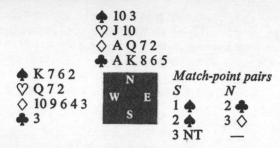

♠ 10 3
♡ J 10
◇ A Q 7 2
♣ A K 8 6 5

♠ K 7 6 2
♡ Q 7 2
◇ 10 9 6 4 3
♣ 3

Match-point pairs

S	*N*
1 ♠	2 ♣
2 ♠	3 ◇
3 NT	—

Favouring the unbid suit, you select the two of hearts as your opening lead. Partner wins with the ace and returns the six, declarer winning with the king. How do you play to this trick?

It is inconceivable that declarer has concealed a five-card heart suit in the bidding, so your partner's six must be his original fourth highest. In that case the Rule of Eleven tells you that declarer has no cards left higher than the six and that it is perfectly safe to unblock by playing your queen to this trick. When declarer subsequently finesses spades you will win at once and lead the seven of hearts so that your partner can make his winners.

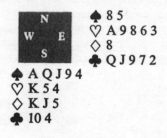

♠ 8 5
♡ A 9 8 6 3
◇ 8
♣ Q J 9 7 2

♠ A Q J 9 4
♡ K 5 4
◇ K J 5
♣ 10 4

Declarer could, of course, have protected his contract by ducking the second round of hearts, but in a pairs game that would have been poor play. He was correct in going up with the king and trying for twelve tricks.

On some hands where you have no use for the Rule of Eleven as such, the knowledge that partner has led his fourth highest card from a long suit can still provide you with a complete blueprint of the distribution.

♠ A 10
♡ 10 8 7 3
◇ A Q J 10 6
♣ 8 2

♠ 9 8 6 5 4 2
♡ Q 6 4 2
◇ 4 3
♣ Q

	N	S
	1 ◇	3 NT

Not fancying the chances of establishing your weak major suits, you try an opening lead of the four of diamonds, regretting it as soon as you see dummy. The ten is played from the table and partner contributes the two. A heart is led to declarer's knave and your queen, and you now try a spade which is won by your partner's king. East returns the three of spades on which South plays the knave under dummy's ace. The ace and king of hearts are cashed, partner throwing the three of clubs, and a diamond to dummy's knave is won by partner's king. East returns the four of clubs, declarer plays the ten and you are in with the queen. What do you lead now?

Has partner underled the ace of clubs? In that case a spade return could be fatal. If, instead, you put dummy in with the heart, partner will make his ace of clubs at the end. But wait a minute. Partner discarded the three of clubs and then led the four. That must mean that he started with only five clubs. You know he had two spades and two hearts, so he must have had four diamonds and dummy is now stone dead. It is hard to believe that declarer, holding only two diamonds, would butcher the hand in this fashion but, if you trust your partner, you must now lead a spade.

♠ K 3
♡ 9 5
◇ K 9 7 2
♣ K J 7 4 3

♠ Q J 7
♡ A K J
◇ 8 5
♣ A 10 9 6 5

It is not only at no trump contracts that the lead of fourth highest can prove of value.

```
                    ♠ J 10 3
                    ♡ 5 4
                    ◇ A 7 6 2
                    ♣ K Q 8 6
 S    W    N    E                  ♠ 8 7 5
 1♠   2♡   2♠   3♡                 ♡ A Q 2
 —    —    3♠   All pass           ◇ J 5 3
                                   ♣ 10 7 5 4
```

West leads the eight of hearts against South's three spade contract. How do you plan the defence?

Is there a chance of defeating this contract? Perhaps, if partner has just the right cards. He will need to have a trump trick and you will have to scrape together four tricks in the red suits. In order to do that it may be necessary to lead diamonds twice from your hand. Now you know from your partner's lead of the eight of hearts that South holds one higher card in the suit but it cannot be the king, for with a suit headed by J 10 9 8 partner would have led the knave. You can therefore safely win the first trick with the queen of hearts, which gives you the necessary entries to attack diamonds.

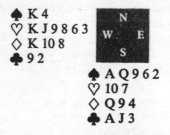

```
♠ K 4
♡ K J 9 8 6 3
◇ K 10 8
♣ 9 2
              ♠ A Q 9 6 2
              ♡ 10 7
              ◇ Q 9 4
              ♣ A J 3
```

It is true that the contract might still be defeated if you win the first trick with the ace of hearts, but that makes the defence much more difficult for your partner. He will need to have nerves of steel to underlead his king of hearts on the second round.

```
                    ♠ A Q 8 3
                    ♡ 9 5 4
                    ◇ 10 6
                    ♣ K J 6 2
   ♠ 9 6 5                        S      W    N    E
   ♡ K 8 3                       5 ◇     —    —    —
   ◇ Q 4
   ♣ A Q 9 8 5
```

You lead the three of hearts against South's five-diamond contract. East wins with the ace and returns the knave on which declarer plays the queen. How should you continue?

Should you carry on with hearts or was declarer's queen a doubleton? Perhaps you should try to set up a spade trick for your partner, but declarer could have a singleton king. Then should you cash the ace of clubs before South's club loser goes away? Fine, if you are sure he has a club loser.

In this situation it may seem that there is very little to guide you, but, in fact, a negative inference is simply screaming to be picked up. If your partner had five hearts he would know declarer had no more than two. The question of trapping the queen would not arise and he would have returned his fourth highest heart to give you a count.

The correct defence, therefore, is to continue with a third round of hearts. Partner will play a fourth round and declarer will be two down.

```
                        ♠ J 10 7 4 2
                        ♡ A J 10 6
                        ◇
                        ♣ 10 7 4 3
            ♠ K
            ♡ Q 7 2
            ◇ A K J 9 8 7 5 3 2
            ♣ —
```

The most widely used defensive signal is undoubtedly the echo, or high-low signal, indicating a liking for the suit partner has led. As with all signals, there is plenty of scope for the exercise of judgement by both defenders.

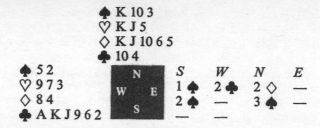

♠ K 10 3
♡ K J 5
◇ K J 10 6 5
♣ 10 4

♠ 5 2
♡ 9 7 3
◇ 8 4
♣ A K J 9 6 2

N
W E
S

S	*W*	*N*	*E*
1♠	2♣	2◇	—
2♠	—	3♠	—
—	—		

On your lead of the ace of clubs your partner plays the eight and declarer the five. How do you continue?

Partner would not echo with queen and two others, for he cannot wish to be on lead against that dummy. If his eight is a singleton declarer has played an improbable false card. Most likely partner has 8 3 in clubs and he will presumably have a trump holding that will be worth a trick if clubs are continued, something like Q J or J 9 8.

However, partner will also need to have ace and queen in one of the red suits if this contract is to be defeated, so it is your duty to switch. Dummy's diamonds are clearly more likely to provide South with discards than hearts, so the heart switch is the best bet. Your lead of the seven of hearts makes sure that the defenders' tricks are taken in the right order.

N
W E
S

♠ J 9 8
♡ A Q 6 4
◇ 9 7 3 2
♣ 8 3

♠ A Q 7 6 4
♡ 10 8 2
◇ A Q
♣ Q 7 5

Some defenders in the East position might refrain from echoing in clubs in order to indicate a switch, but this could lead to misdefence. After cashing his two heart tricks East would return the eight of clubs on which South might well play the queen. West could then decide to exit safely in hearts in the hope that his partner will make a trick in trumps or diamonds.

Defenders must acquire the habit of signalling to show their distribution whenever they may safely do so. It is conventional to echo with two or four cards in the suit led and to play low-high with three. This can be a valuable aid to counting in both suit and no trump contracts. It is particularly useful when there is a long suit in dummy.

♠ A 4
♡ 8 7 2
◇ 10 6 3
♣ K Q J 9 4

S	N		♠ K 9 3
1 ♡	2 ♣		♡ Q 10 9 6 3
2 NT	3 ♡		◇ J 5
3 NT	—		♣ A 10 8

West leads the five of spades against South's three no trump contract. The four is played from dummy and you win with the king and return the nine to dummy's ace. On the king of clubs you play the eight, South the two and partner the three. What do you do when the queen of clubs is now led?

Yes, of course, you win with your ace and lead your last spade, for your partner's three on the first round of clubs told you he had three cards in the suit and declarer only two.

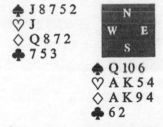

♠ J 8 7 5 2
♡ J
◇ Q 8 7 2
♣ 7 5 3

♠ Q 10 6
♡ A K 5 4
◇ A K 9 4
♣ 6 2

Note that South could have given you a guess by playing his six of clubs on the first round, for then your partner's three might for all you know be the start of an echo from 3 2. If declarer had succeeded in slipping through a second club trick he would have made his contract by playing on diamonds.

```
            ♠ J 10 7 2
            ♥ K 8 3
            ♦ K J 4
            ♣ Q J 10
  ♠ K Q 9 6                    S        N
  ♥ 7 6                       2 ♥      3 NT
  ♦ A 8 5 3                   4 ♣      4 ♥
  ♣ 8 4 3                     6 ♥      —
```

You lead the king of spades against South's contract of six hearts, partner following with the eight and declarer winning with the ace. At trick two South leads the nine of diamonds. Quick! What do you do?

It is one of those awkward occasions when you may need time for thought, but cannot afford to take it. Your reaction must be lightning swift, for if you have not by now played low with the proper degree of indifference you have given away the slam. The clue, of course, is partner's eight of spades which tells you that he has an even number of cards in the suit. Could it be two? Surely not, for if declarer's hand were ♠ A x x, ♥ A Q J 10 x, ♦ 9, ♣ A K x x, he would hardly have an opening two bid. Partner was showing four spades then and declarer's ace was single. It is too much to hope that your partner has a trick in trumps or clubs, so the only chance is for the defenders to make two diamond tricks.

```
                        ♠ 8 5 4 3
                        ♥ 9 2
                        ♦ Q 10 7 6
                        ♣ 6 5 2
            ♠ A
            ♥ A Q J 10 5 4
            ♦ 9 2
            ♣ A K 9 7
```

It is vital to play without the slightest hesitation in such situations. If you do not have time to analyse the position you must play by instinct and *you must play quickly*. A quick mistake is much more easily forgiven than a give-away pause.

Another invaluable defensive aid is the trump echo. This is used in the opposite way to the echo in a side suit. In trumps it is conventional to echo when holding three cards and to play low-high with two or four.

There is some divergence of opinion in expert circles as to how the trump echo should be used. One school of thought holds that a trump echo should not be made unless you wish to convey to your partner your ability to ruff some outside suit. This method has the advantage of clarity and simplicity, but it is needlessly rigid. The better way, when playing with a thinking and counting partner, is to echo to show three trumps whenever you can safely do so. The operative word is 'safely', for some discretion must be used here. It would obviously be foolish, for instance, to use the echo when holding an honour card, as in the East hand below.

$$A\,7\,4$$

$$Q \qquad\qquad J\,6\,2$$

$$K\,10\,9\,8\,5\,3$$

When the ace is played on the first round East should follow with the two. Another case where it would be wiser not to echo is when your partner may have a doubleton queen of trumps.

$$K\,J\,5\,4$$

$$7\,6\,3 \qquad\qquad Q\,2$$

$$A\,10\,9\,8$$

On the lead of the ace by South, West should play the three.

From time to time hands may crop up where there is a serious danger that the partner might, erroneously, place you with a void in a side suit and try to give you a ruff. Here, too, it is as well to refrain from echoing even if you have three trumps as a warning to partner that you cannot ruff.

But on the vast majority of hands in which you have three small trumps it will be perfectly safe for you to echo, and in a number of cases that will be all the help partner needs to enable him to find the killing defence.

♠ K J 8 7
♡ K 10 4 2
◇ J 6
♣ K 9 3

♠ 5
♡ Q 8 3
◇ K 10 7 5 2
♣ 10 7 6 4

S		N	
1 ♠		3 ♠	
6 ♣		—	

Against this uninformative bidding you lead, with some trepidation, the five of diamonds. Partner obligingly produces the queen and declarer wins with the ace. The ace of trumps is followed by a small trump to the king, partner playing the four and then the two. Next comes a club to South's ace, a club back to dummy's king and a third round of clubs which declarer ruffs. South now exits with the nine of diamonds to your king. What do you lead?

Aren't you grateful to your partner for giving you the count? You know that declarer started with only five trumps. If he has no more diamonds he must have four hearts, so a diamond return is perfectly safe. Without the trump echo you would have to assume that declarer had six trumps and therefore only three red cards left. You would try the lead of the queen of hearts, which might or might not deceive the declarer.

♠ 4 3 2
♡ J 6
◇ Q 8 4 3
♣ Q J 8 5

♠ A Q 10 9 6
♡ A 9 7 5
◇ A 9
♣ A 2

A defensive lead convention that is not as widely known as it deserves to be rejoices in the unromantic name of MUD. The initials stand for middle, up, down, and the convention is used in defending against suit contracts when leading from a worthless trebleton, three cards not headed by an honour. When you wish to lead from a holding of something like 9 7 3, as in the hand on page 34, you lead the middle card and follow on the second round with the higher one. The main advantage of this signal is that it makes it easy for your partner to distinguish between your doubleton and trebleton leads. All is clear by the second round. Indeed when the card you lead is the highest of the outstanding small cards partner can recognize the lead for a doubleton straightaway.

```
              ♠ K 10 9 4
              ♡ A 7 5 2
              ◇ Q 8 4
              ♣ Q 9
  S     N                    ♠ A Q 6 5
  1 ♡   3 ♡          N       ♡ 8
  4 ♡   —        W       E   ◇ J 9 7 3
                    S       ♣ 10 8 6 4
```

Your partner leads the ace of diamonds (A from A K) against South's four heart call, and then switches to the eight of spades. If you are playing MUD the way to defeat the contract is immediately clear, for partner would not have led the eight from a trebleton.

```
  ♠ 8 7
  ♡ J 6              N
  ◇ A K 10 6 5   W       E
  ♣ J 7 5 2          S
              ♠ J 3 2
              ♡ K Q 10 9 4 3
              ◇ 2
              ♣ A K 3
```

Without the help of MUD you could go wrong here. If South plays a deceptive knave on the second round of spades you may be tempted to try for another diamond trick.

The suit preference signals devised by Hy Lavinthal over thirty years ago form an important part of the defensive arsenal and are used by good players all over the world. Suit preference signals can be given either when leading or in following suit. Used properly, they do not clash with any of the standard signals. Lavinthal discards, being more controversial in nature, are not so widely accepted and have no place in this book.

				♠ K Q 9 4
				♡ K 3
				◇ 7
				♣ A Q 10 8 6 3

W	N	E	S	♠ 2
—	1 ♣	—	1 ♠	♡ A J 7
Dbl.	4 ♠	5 ◇	—	◇ J 9 6 5 3
—	5 ♠	Dbl.	All pass	♣ K J 7 4

After some vigorous competitive bidding, your partner leads the ace of diamonds against South's doubled contract of five spades. How do you defend?

It is quite clear that any club losers that declarer may have cannot disappear, but if your partner has the queen of hearts you will require an immediate heart lead from him to obtain the maximum penalty. How can you give partner the message? Quite simply, by playing your knave of diamonds on the first trick. This, being an unnecessarily high card, will be clearly recognizable as a Lavinthal suit preference signal asking for a heart switch.

♠ 6 3
♡ Q 8 6 5 4
◇ A K 8 4 2
♣ 5

♠ A J 10 8 7 5
♡ 10 9 2
◇ Q 10
♣ 9 2

That is a fairly straightfoward example of the use of the suit preference signal but sometimes, as in the next hand, it is not too easy to determine which suit you should ask your partner to switch to.

```
                    ♠ —
                    ♡ K Q 7 2
                    ◇ K J 4
                    ♣ K Q 8 7 5 2
♠ A 3                              Game all
♡ A 8 6 5 3        N
◇ A 9 7 3 2      W   E    S   W   N   E
♣ 9                S      3♠  —   —   —
```

You lead the ace of diamonds against South's three spade contract, your partner following with the queen and declarer with the five. What do you lead now?

Your opening lead has turned out well and it is up to you to make the most of it. It looks natural to lead the nine of diamonds as a Lavinthal asking for a heart return, but a little counting shows that this can hardly be right. With at least seven spades and four diamonds, South can have only two cards in the other two suits. If one of them is a heart the contract will always be defeated by two tricks and there is no hurry to make your ace of hearts. If South should happen to have two clubs, however, it will be essential for you to obtain a club ruff. You should therefore lead the two of diamonds to ask for a club return.

Partner ruffs and duly returns a small club which South wins with the ace. You play the ace on South's knave of spades and lead the three of diamonds as a repeat Lavinthal, confirming that your club was a singleton and that you have a trump to ruff with. Your partner can now work out the position for himself. He will know that you have the ace of hearts, and if he started with five clubs he will ignore your signal and lead a heart.

```
                    ♠ 9 7 6 2
        N           ♡ J 10 9 4
      W   E         ◇ Q
        S           ♣ J 10 4 3
            ♠ K Q J 10 8 5 4
            ♡ —
            ◇ 10 8 6 5
            ♣ A 6
```

Note that a heart lead from East at trick three would allow the declarer to make his contract.

Here is a hand from a pairs contest where the suit preference signal came a trick too late.

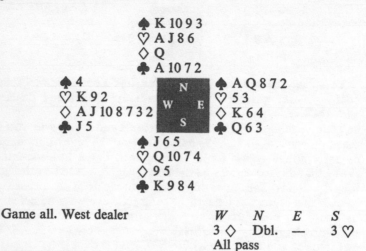

♠ K 10 9 3
♡ A J 8 6
◇ Q
♣ A 10 7 2

♠ 4
♡ K 9 2
◇ A J 10 8 7 3 2
♣ J 5

♠ A Q 8 7 2
♡ 5 3
◇ K 6 4
♣ Q 6 3

♠ J 6 5
♡ Q 10 7 4
◇ 9 5
♣ K 9 8 4

Game all. West dealer

W	N	E	S
3 ◇	Dbl.	—	3 ♡
All pass			

West led the four of spades, the three was played from dummy and East won with the queen. East continued with the ace of spades, West throwing his small club, and then the eight of spades which West ruffed. West now led the knave of diamonds to his partner's king and a fourth round of spades was ruffed by South's ten and over-ruffed by the king. When South got in he drew trumps, played a club to the ace and finessed against East's queen of clubs to make eight tricks altogether. Plus 100 was a poor result for East-West, for most pairs made nine tricks in diamonds for a score of 110.

What went wrong? Clearly the contract would have gone two down if West had not discarded his small club at trick two, but, as West pointed out in the post-mortem, he did not know where his partner's entry lay at that stage and had made the discard that was sure to defeat the contract whichever minor king East held. It was conceivable that South's hand was something like ♠ J x x x, ♡ Q 10 x x x, ◇ K x x, ♣ Q, in which case West must discard a club to defeat the contract.

If East had exercised a little imagination he might have foreseen that the play of the ace of spades could give West an awkward choice of discards. A player accustomed to anticipating his partner's problems would have made his Lavinthal by leading the eight of spades at trick two. Then the road to a top score would have been clear.

All players who wish to improve their defence must acquire the habit of considering their partners' problems at every stage and making the play that gives partner the least opportunity of going wrong. This theme is of such importance that it will have a later chapter all to itself.

3 • More Counting

Have you ever had the chastening experience of waking up in the middle of a hand to the realization that you are defending solely by instinct, that you have neglected to count and have no clear idea of what is going on? It has certainly happened to me, and I suspect it has happened to you.

The instinct of an experienced defender is, of course, quite highly developed and will keep you on the right road most of the time, but once in a while it will lead you into an error that could have been avoided if you had been keeping a careful count. How can a defender learn to avoid these occasional, costly aberrations?

I suggest that you practise counting suit distributions whenever you have a spare moment. If you have difficulty in sleeping at night, instead of counting sheep or creditors or master points, try counting suit distributions. Start with any number from four to ten and repeat to yourself all the complementary combinations of numbers that add up to thirteen. It is best to do this out loud but, if you think your dear ones may sit on your head and send for a strait-jacket, you can do it mentally. You should aim to reach a point where, under the stimulus of the number six, your brain will fire back with computer-like precision the series 7-0-0, 6-1-0, 5-2-0, 5-1-1, 4-3-0, 4-2-1, 3-3-1, 3-2-2.

Doing this homework in advance is likely to pay big dividends at the bridge table. There are many demands on your concentration when you are defending, and your whole game will benefit if you can make the process of counting as automatic as possible.

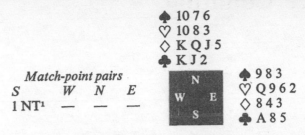

♠ 10 7 6
♡ 10 8 3
◇ K Q J 5
♣ K J 2

Match-point pairs

S	W	N	E
1 NT[1]	—	—	—

♠ 9 8 3
♡ Q 9 6 2
◇ 8 4 3
♣ A 8 5

Your partner leads the ten of clubs and the knave is played from dummy. Since you do not wish to expend at this stage what is probably your only entry, you encourage with the eight. A spade is led from dummy and declarer's queen wins the trick. Next comes the six of diamonds. West plays the two and dummy's knave wins, and a further spade is led to declarer's knave. Partner produces the king and leads the queen of clubs, covered by dummy's king and your ace. How should you continue?

On the play of the spades declarer is marked with the ace. Your partner's two of diamonds makes it likely that declarer has that ace as well (his no trump bid would be very lop-sided without it, anyway). That accounts for eleven of declarer's points, so he cannot have more than the king in hearts. You should therefore lead the queen of hearts to give South a guess. If he guesses wrong, playing you for the heart knave as well, he will go one down in his contract in spite of his twenty-four points.

♠ K 5 4
♡ A J 4
◇ 10 9 2
♣ Q 10 9 6

♠ A Q J 2
♡ K 7 5
◇ A 7 6
♣ 7 4 3

[1] 12–14 points.

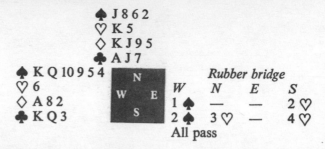

```
              ♠ J 8 6 2
              ♡ K 5
              ◇ K J 9 5
              ♣ A J 7
♠ K Q 10 9 5 4                    Rubber bridge
♡ 6            N
◇ A 8 2      W   E      W    N    E    S
♣ K Q 3        S        1 ♠   —    —    2 ♡
                        2 ♠   3 ♡   —    4 ♡
                        All pass
```

You lead the king of spades against South's contract of four hearts. East follows with the three and South with the seven. How should you continue?

Once again, this is a simple matter of counting points. If your partner passed your opening bid with the ace of spades in his hand he cannot have as much as a queen outside. You cannot hope for two diamond tricks in that case, and you cannot expect your partner to have a trump trick, for South must be fairly long in trumps to compensate for his lack of honour strength. The only chance of defeating the contract is to make two tricks in clubs. You should lead the three in the hope that your partner has the ten and that declarer will make the wrong guess.

```
              N          ♠ A 3
            W   E        ♡ 10 7 3
              S          ◇ 7 6 4 3
                         ♣ 10 5 4 2
        ♠ 7
        ♡ A Q J 9 8 4 2
        ◇ Q 10
        ♣ 9 8 6
```

Declarer should not make the wrong guess, of course, for the inferences from your partner's pass are equally available to him. But he may suspect your king of spades of being a deceptive lead from ace, king, or he may just neglect to count. Declarers do sometimes.

In a pairs game your proper lead at trick two would be the club king, for you could not risk giving South an easy overtrick.

♠ 9 4
♡ A Q 10 8 5 2
◇ K J 7
♣ 8 6

S	N
1 ♠	2 ♡
3 ◇	3 ♡
4 ◇	5 ◇

♠ Q 5
♡ J 9 6 4
◇ 10 9 2
♣ A K 9 3

Your partner leads the four of clubs to your king and South plays the seven. How should you continue?

You know from the bidding that South has at least five spades and five diamonds. The club lead marks him with two cards in that suit, therefore he has at most a singleton heart. His honour cards are probably ace and king of spades and ace and queen of diamonds. If he has six spades headed by ace and king you are not going to defeat this contract, for the spades will be set up by ruffing with an honour in dummy. Suppose declarer has five spades and a singleton heart. Now the heart suit represents a threat. On any passive return South will be able to ruff out the hearts and come to eleven tricks that way. Then the best defence must be to play a forcing game and continue with ace and another club. There can be no danger in conceding a ruff and discard even in the unlikely event that South is lacking the king of spades. He will have entry trouble no matter which hand he ruffs in.

♠ J 10 7 2
♡ K 7
◇ 8 3
♣ Q 10 5 4 2

♠ A K 8 6 3
♡ 3
◇ A Q 6 5 4
♣ J 7

With West holding the eight of trumps, there is no way for South to make eleven tricks after a third round of clubs.

```
              ♠ 10
              ♡ K 9 3
              ◇ K Q 6 4
              ♣ 10 9 7 4 2
   ♠ Q 9 5 4 3                    S      N
   ♡ A J 6      N              1 ♠    1 NT
   ◇ A 9 8    W   E            3 ♣    4 ♣
   ♣ 8 3        S              4 ♠    5 ♣
```

You lead the ace of diamonds against South's five club contract,
East playing the three and declarer the two. How should you
continue?

Prospects do not look very bright, for South will not be missing
three aces on this bidding. The position is hopeless if South has
five clubs headed by the ace. Even if he has only four clubs with
the ace and king he will make his contract by drawing trumps in
two rounds, leading a heart to the king and then cross-ruffing.
Then you must assume partner's clubs to be as good as king and
another. Declarer will need an entry to dummy to finesse trumps.
He will have no difficulty if he has another diamond, but he may
now be void in diamonds. Quite a likely distribution for South is
6-2-1-4, in which case East will have a singleton spade and declarer will be unable to enter dummy by means of a second round
spade ruff. Then it looks as though you should lead a spade now
to prepare the way for an over-ruff by partner. So you should, but
there is a further danger. The odds are against partner's singleton
spade being an honour card. If it is not, dummy's ten could provide the entry declarer needs, allowing him to discard his heart
losers on the diamonds and then finesse in trumps for an overtrick
To guard against this you must lead the queen of spades at trick
two.

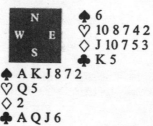

```
              N              ♠ 6
            W   E            ♡ 10 8 7 4 2
              S              ◇ J 10 7 5 3
                             ♣ K 5
         ♠ A K J 8 7 2
         ♡ Q 5
         ◇ 2
         ♣ A Q J 6
```

♠ K J 10 7
♡ K Q 3
◇ A K 8 6
♣ 6 2

♠ A 8 5 3 2
♡ 7
◇ J 9 7 4
♣ J 10 3

N	S
1 ♠	2 ♡
3 ♡	4 ♡

West leads the four of spades against South's contract of four hearts. You win with the ace and declarer plays the nine. How do you plan the defence?

Your partner would not attack the suit North bid by leading from a holding of Q 6 4. In spite of South's play of the nine it is clear that partner has led a singleton and you can now give him a ruff. But should you give him a ruff straightaway? You need four tricks to set this contract, and the other two will obviously have to come from clubs. That means partner's clubs must be as good as A K or A Q. The second holding is more likely, for with A K partner might well have led the ace originally. At all events it must be right to lead the club knave at trick two. If the knave is allowed to hold the trick you will immediately switch back to spades to give partner his ruff. If your club knave is covered by declarer, partner will have to show a little faith and underlead his remaining honour card to put you in.

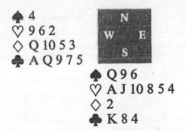

♠ 4
♡ 9 6 2
◇ Q 10 5 3
♣ A Q 9 7 5

♠ Q 9 6
♡ A J 10 8 5 4
◇ 2
♣ K 8 4

If clubs are not attacked at trick two, declarer will be able to discard two of his clubs on dummy's winners.

♠ 9 6 3
♡ A 5
◇ A Q 9 8 4
♣ Q 8 2

♠ J 8 7 4
♡ J 3
◇ 10 6 2
♣ A J 5 3

S	N
1 NT[1]	3 NT

Against South's three no trump contract you lead the four of spades. Your partner plays the king and South wins with the ace. Declarer immediately returns the two of spades. What do you make of that?

For South's play to make any sense his original spade holding must have been A Q 10 2. It is ominous that the declarer has not attacked diamonds. If the diamonds were in need of development declarer would not be trying to promote a single extra spade trick at this stage. The only logical conclusion is that the diamonds are solid. Then declarer has six tricks in the red suits plus two tricks already established in spades. The nine of spades, if he is allowed to make it, will be his ninth trick. You must therefore go up with your knave of spades and rely on making four club tricks to defeat the contract.

Your partner's club holding will have to be as good as K 10 x or K 9 x x. To cater for both possibilities you must lead the knave.

♠ K 5
♡ K 9 8 6 2
◇ 7 3
♣ K 9 7 4

♠ A Q 10 2
♡ Q 10 7 4
◇ K J 5
♣ 10 6

[1] 12–14 points.

♠ J 7 6
♡ K 8 3
◇ Q 10 5 4
♣ A Q 7

S	N		♠ Q 5 3
1 ♡	2 NT		♡ 7 2
4 ♡	—		◇ K 9 6 2
			♣ J 10 6 4

West leads the ten of spades, the six is played from dummy, you follow with the five and South wins with the ace. The ace of hearts is cashed and a small heart is led to dummy's king, your partner following both times. The four of diamonds is now led from dummy. How do you plan the defence?

A simple count of declarer's tricks will save you from going wrong. On the bidding South is marked with six heart winners, he has already made the ace of spades and you can see that he can make two club tricks by finessing. That adds up to nine, and if declarer can make a further trick in either diamonds or spades he will be home. Your correct play, therefore, is to go up with your king of diamonds and continue with spades.

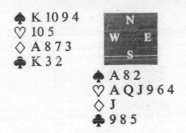

♠ K 10 9 4
♡ 10 5
◇ A 8 7 3
♣ K 3 2

♠ A 8 2
♡ A Q J 9 6 4
◇ J
♣ 9 8 5

Observe that if you had played low on the diamond trick partner would have had to win with the ace. Declarer would then have been able to trump-finesse diamonds through your king and obtain a discard of his losing club.

Although three no trumps is a lucky make on the hand, it is hard to fault South's bidding. He would have made four hearts against most defenders, anyway.

```
                    ♠ 7 6 3
                    ♡ 8 5 2
                    ◇ Q J 7 5 4
                    ♣ A J
  ♠ 9 8 4        N          S        N
  ♡ 10 6                    1 ♠      2 ◇
  ◇ A 10 8 6 2   W    E     3 NT     —
  ♣ K 8 3          S
```

On your lead of ten of hearts East plays the seven and South the king. A club is led and dummy's knave wins and the club ace is cashed. A spade is led to South's queen and the queen of clubs puts you in. How should you continue?

If declarer has four clubs he is likely to have five spades, and his spades must be solid otherwise he would not be messing about with clubs. If declarer has the ace of hearts he is clearly going to make ten tricks. His original heart holding could have been K Q x, however. That would leave him with a singleton diamond which is certainly not the king since he did not attack the suit. In that case the best line of defence is clear. The ace of diamonds followed by a small one to your partner's king will force declarer to throw a winning spade in order to keep a heart guard. Partner will exit in a black suit and make his ace and knave of hearts at the end.

```
        N          ♠ 10 5
                   ♡ A J 9 7 4
    W       E      ◇ K 9
                   ♣ 9 6 5 2
          S
    ♠ A K Q J 2
    ♡ K Q 3
    ◇ 3
    ♣ Q 10 7 4
```

When this hand turned up in the Eastbourne Spring Foursomes in 1964, most of the West players went wrong. So did the declarers, of course, for the chosen line of play cannot possibly gain if the defence is accurate. The only real chance for the declarer is to try for a second heart trick when in dummy with the knave of clubs.

♠ 9 4
♡ A 8 6 5
◇ K Q 9 3
♣ K Q 7

S	N
1 ♡	4 ♣
6 ♡	—

♠ K J 6 2
♡ K 7
◇ 7 6
♣ 10 9 6 4 3

North's four club bid is the Swiss Convention, showing a hand worth a raise to four hearts and strong in high cards.

Your partner leads the three of spades against South's slam. Not many partners underlead aces against slam contracts so, since you would like to know who has the queen of spades, you put in the knave. South has the queen and wins the trick with it. Now comes the queen of hearts on which your partner plays the nine and dummy the five. What do you play after taking your king of hearts?

It is clear that you have to find your partner's ace, and this is a situation where many players go wrong for want of a little counting. South is known to have three spades and not more than six hearts. He therefore has at least four cards in the minor suits. If he has a losing diamond he will not be able to dispose of it, but a losing club might well be thrown on dummy's fourth diamond. The club return is marked.

♠ 10 8 7 3
♡ 9
◇ 10 8 4 2
♣ A J 5 2

♠ A Q 5
♡ Q J 10 4 3 2
◇ A J 5
♣ 8

On a strictly percentage basis declarer's best play is to cash the ace of hearts first. If the king does not drop he still has the chance that the defender who holds it will have to follow to three rounds of diamonds. But South probably reckoned that the chances of a defensive slip more than corrected the balance in favour of the finesse.

Your partner leads the two of spades and the five is played from dummy. How do you plan the defence?

It is likely that West has led from the ace of spades, for otherwise dummy's queen would have been played. If declarer has the knave of spades and the ace of hearts, it would be fatal for you to play the ten on this trick. That would limit the defenders' tricks to three spades and the king of clubs. Hearts offer the only possible source of extra tricks. You must play your king of spades and lead the nine of hearts. If declarer wins this heart trick and partner fails to signal for a continuation, you will be able to switch back to spades when in with the club king in the faint hope that partner's spades are headed by the ace and knave.

If declarer plays small on your heart lead, your partner, on winning with the knave, will not be in doubt as to how to continue. Knowing that you will have to have the king of clubs, he will reason that the only chance of a further trick is in spades. He will lead the seven in the hope that your original spade holding was either K x x x or K 10 x.

4 · Breaking Ground

The selection of the initial lead is often the most vital and the most difficult decision that a defender has to make, and more tricks are thrown away here than in any other phase of defence. The reason is plain enough. The opening leader is operating in the dark with just two things to guide him—the bidding and the cards in his own hand. From the correlation of this scanty data he must arrive at a decision that will influence the entire conduct of the defence. No wonder he sometimes starts off on the wrong foot.

It is dangerous to be dogmatic on this subject, for nobody can hope to find the killing lead every time. The most expert of defenders expects to present declarer with a trick, or even the contract, once in a while. All we can do is try, in a given set of circumstances, to find the lead that will produce good results on balance.

The standard table of leads from honour sequences is well enough known and need not be reproduced here. As you will have observed from some of the earlier hands, I favour the modern lead of the ace rather than the king from a suit headed by both top honours. The removal of ambiguity from the lead of the king resolves partner's doubts when he has the critical holdings of x x, or J x x, in the suit. This is not a vital matter, however, and many players prefer to stick to the familiar lead of the king.

Since it is impossible to recommend opening leads in the abstract, let us look at some hands and bidding sequences.

♠ J 10 6		S	N
♡ A 7 3	N	1 NT	3 NT
◇ J 9 6 4 3	W E		
♣ 8 2	S		

It is normally correct to lead from length against no trump contracts, and here you have no reason to choose anything other than your fourth highest diamond. Substitute a small heart for the ace, however, and the diamond lead becomes pointless. With a virtually entry-less hand you will do better to abandon diamonds

55

and try the knave of spades, hoping to develop the suit for your partner.

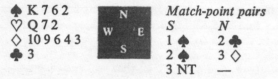

♠ J 7 6 2
♡ K 8 5
◇ 9 4
♣ Q 10 7 3

	S	N
	1 ♡	2 ◇
	2 NT	3 ♡
	3 NT	—

The choice between two four-card suits can be difficult. Other things being equal, it is usually better to open the major suit, but here the texture of your spades is too thin and the club lead is preferable. Any club honour in your partner's hand will help to establish the suit.

♠ K 7 6 2
♡ Q 7 2
◇ 10 9 6 4 3
♣ 3

Match-point pairs

S	N
1 ♠	2 ♣
2 ♠	3 ◇
3 NT	—

Here the attack on the unbid suit is superior to any other choice. Although the lead of the two from a three-card suit may mislead partner on occasion, it can also deceive declarer. This, you will remember, was one of the hands in Chapter Two, and no other lead had any chance of defeating the contract.

When the declarer, in good faith, has bid your best suit, it is obviously advisable to try something else as an opening lead.

♠ K J 9 5 2
♡ 9 8
◇ A 8 3
♣ 7 6 4

S	N
1 ♠	2 ♣
2 NT	3 NT

The usual rule in leading from short suits is to prefer a major to a minor and a trebleton to a doubleton. Here the decision is extremely close. If a panel of experts were polled I would expect the nine of hearts to win by a narrow margin from the three of diamonds. Either lead makes a reasonable start for the defence and the contract will be defeated if the defenders are on their toes, for the full hand is as follows:

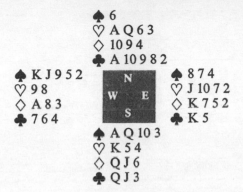

```
              ♠ 6
              ♡ A Q 6 3
              ◇ 10 9 4
              ♣ A 10 9 8 2
  ♠ K J 9 5 2      N       ♠ 8 7 4
  ♡ 9 8                    ♡ J 10 7 2
  ◇ A 8 3       W   E      ◇ K 7 5 2
  ♣ 7 6 4          S       ♣ K 5
              ♠ A Q 10 3
              ♡ K 5 4
              ◇ Q J 6
              ♣ Q J 3
```

Leading against no trumps is a simple matter compared with leading against a suit contract. The introduction of the element of trumps means that the opening leader has a wider range of strategic choice, and therefore more scope for error.

Given the right conditions, a trump lead can have a devastating effect, but you must listen to the bidding with a delicate ear to determine whether the right conditions obtain. You can usually tell when declarer is likely to be able to use dummy's trumps for ruffing, or when he will play a cross-ruff.

```
  ♠ Q J 7 3      N        S         N
  ♡ A Q 10                1 ♡       1 NT
  ◇ 7 5 2      W   E      2 ♣       —
  ♣ 10 8 4        S
```

When you lead a trump you are, in effect, trying to play the hand at no trumps. Obviously one of the best times to do that is when you have a balanced distribution with your honours favourably placed, as in the above case. Declarer has told you he is unbalanced and dummy is likely to be short in hearts, so the lead of the four of clubs is marked.

When one of the opponents rejects the opportunity to play in no trumps, a trump lead is usually indicated.

		S	N
		1 ♠	2 ♠
		2 NT	4 ♠

North advertised his ruffing values by preferring the higher level spade game, so you should lead a trump.

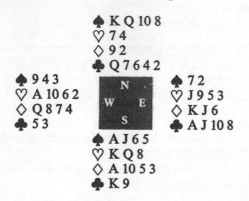

On any other lead South will make ten tricks by setting up dummy's club suit.

♠ K J 7 6 2
♡ A 8 3
◇ 9 4
♣ 10 8 6

S	N
1 ◇	1 ♡
2 ♣	3 ◇
5 ◇	—

The opponents have again avoided no trumps, but a trump lead would be highly dangerous against this bidding. The difference is that both North and South have bid side suits, and there is a serious risk of your spade tricks disappearing if the suit is not attacked. The spade six is the proper lead.

♠ 10 8 3
♡ Q J 10 7 5
◇ K J 8 3
♣ K

♠ K J 7 6 2   ♠ A 9 5
♡ A 8 3   ♡ K 9 4 2
◇ 9 4   ◇ 7 2
♣ 10 8 6   ♣ 7 5 4 3

♠ Q 4
♡ 6
◇ A Q 10 6 5
♣ A Q J 9 2

A passive trump lead would allow declarer to make twelve tricks.

♠ 10 9 2
♡ K 7 5
◇ 10 6 5
♣ K 10 6 3

N	S
1 ♠	2 ♣
2 ◇	2 ♡
2 NT	3 ◇
3 ♡	4 ♡

When the opponents land in a four-three fit after bidding every suit a trump is often the best lead. In this case, South clearly hopes to be able to play some sort of cross-ruff, or else he would have chosen the nine-trick game.

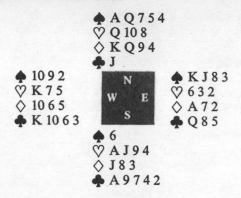

♠ A Q 7 5 4
♡ Q 10 8
◇ K Q 9 4
♣ J

♠ 10 9 2
♡ K 7 5
◇ 10 6 5
♣ K 10 6 3

♠ K J 8 3
♡ 6 3 2
◇ A 7 2
♣ Q 8 5

♠ 6
♡ A J 9 4
◇ J 8 3
♣ A 9 7 4 2

After an initial trump lead best defence will hold declarer to nine tricks.

♠ A 10 7 3 2
♡ 8 2
◇ 10 5
♣ A 9 6 5

S	N
1 ♠	2 ◇
2 ♠	2 NT
3 ♡	—

The opponents seem to have found a fit of sorts, but this is not the right moment for a trump lead. South is probably 6-4 in the majors, partner will be able to over-ruff dummy and a rollicking defensive cross-ruff may develop. Your most promising lead is the ten of diamonds.

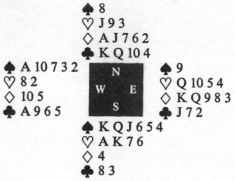

♠ 8
♡ J 9 3
◇ A J 7 6 2
♣ K Q 10 4

♠ A 10 7 3 2
♡ 8 2
◇ 10 5
♣ A 9 6 5

♠ 9
♡ Q 10 5 4
◇ K Q 9 8 3
♣ J 7 2

♠ K Q J 6 5 4
♡ A K 7 6
◇ 4
♣ 8 3

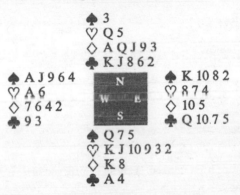

		S	W	N	E
♠ A J 9 6 4		1 ♡	1 ♠	2 ◇	2 ♠
♡ A 6		—	—	3 ♣	—
◇ 7 6 4 2		3 ♡	—	4 ♡	All pass
♣ 9 3					

North has bid two suits and then given delayed support to his partner. He will not have more than one spade, therefore. Dummy's shape could be 1-3-5-4, in which case there is not much hope, but it is rather more likely to be 1-2-5-5. In the latter case the best method of attack is obvious once you think of it. You can extract dummy's trumps while retaining control by the simple expedient of underleading your ace of hearts.

```
              ♠ 3
              ♡ Q 5
              ◇ A Q J 9 3
              ♣ K J 8 6 2
♠ A J 9 6 4                    ♠ K 10 8 2
♡ A 6              N           ♡ 8 7 4
◇ 7 6 4 2      W       E       ◇ 10 5
♣ 9 3              S           ♣ Q 10 7 5
              ♠ Q 7 5
              ♡ K J 10 9 3 2
              ◇ K 8
              ♣ A 4
```

Declarer will eye your six of hearts with little enthusiasm, for he will be unable to make more than nine tricks.

		S	N
♠ K 8 7 2		2 ♡	2 NT
♡ 5		3 ◇	3 ♠
◇ A 7 6 3		4 ◇	4 ♡
♣ K 9 6 4			

There is clearly no point in surrendering a tempo by leading trumps here. Declarer is unlikely to need to ruff diamonds in dummy. But your partner could have four trumps, in which case you may be able to shorten declarer's trumps to the point of embarrassment by forcing him with club leads. You must play for partner to have some strength in clubs and, since South will be short in the suit, you should lead the king.

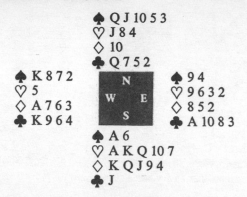

The lead of a singleton can be a very aggressive form of attack, but it is a lead that is frequently overrated. The general rule should be to lead a singleton only when you have a real expectancy of getting a ruff. Otherwise the gain is all declarer's.

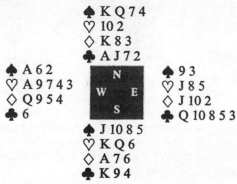

In this case you are too strong in high cards for the singleton lead to have much chance of success. Your partner is unlikely to have that vital entry that will be needed to give you a ruff. A club lead may ruin your partner's holding in the suit and at best will give up a tempo unnecessarily. The four of diamonds is your best bet.

♠ 10
♡ Q J 9 4 2
◇ 9 4 3
♣ Q J 10 3

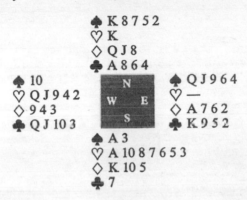

	S	N
	1 ♡	1 ♠
	2 ♡	3 NT
	4 ♡	—

To attack clubs on this hand would be quite the wrong defence. Your trump holding is of the dangerous type that lends itself to a trump endplay. Your immediate aim should be to shorten your trumps and the singleton spade lead is ideal. Partner is likely to have an entry somewhere and you will get your ruff.

```
                    ♣ K 8 7 5 2
                    ♡ K
                    ◇ Q J 8
                    ♣ A 8 6 4
     ♠ 10                              ♠ Q J 9 6 4
     ♡ Q J 9 4 2          N            ♡ —
     ◇ 9 4 3          W       E        ◇ A 7 6 2
     ♣ Q J 10 3           S            ♣ K 9 5 2
                    ♠ A 3
                    ♡ A 10 8 7 6 5 3
                    ◇ K 10 5
                    ♣ 7
```

On any lead other than the spade South can make his contract.

♠ K 8 2
♡ 9 5
◇ J 8 7 3
♣ Q 6 4 2

	S	N
	1 ♠	2 ♣
	2 ♠	3 ♠
	4 ♠	—

Neither minor suit offers an attractive attack, there is no reason to lead a trump and the nine of hearts seems the most promising lead here. A doubleton lead is quite often effective when you have trump control.

Your partner will be able to deduce that you have led from a doubleton, for with four hearts headed by king and queen South would surely have rebid two hearts. East will play the ten on the first trick and you will later get your ruff.

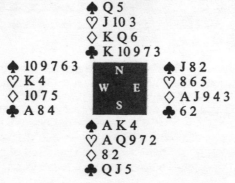

To a defender with a practised ear the thing that stands out about this auction is that partner is unlikely to have more than two clubs. You should prepare a ruff for him by leading the club four.

♠ Q 5
♡ J 10 3
♢ K Q 6
♣ K 10 9 7 3

♠ 10 9 7 6 3   ♠ J 8 2
♡ K 4   ♡ 8 6 5
♢ 10 7 5   ♢ A J 9 4 3
♣ A 8 4   ♣ 6 2

♠ A K 4
♡ A Q 9 7 2
♢ 8 2
♣ Q J 5

On the actual hand the lead of the ace and another club would do just as well, but the underlead is better for reasons of control. Partner might have a doubleton queen or even a singleton king. Should dummy prove to have only four clubs and partner fail to echo, you may still have time to switch and take two tricks in diamonds.

What about this one:

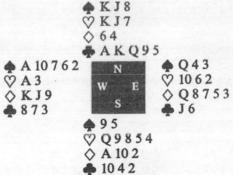

♠ A 10 7 6 2
♡ A 3
◇ K J 9
♣ 8 7 3

N	E	S	W
1♣	—	1♡	1♠
3♡	—	4♡	All pass

Many players still retain a strong prejudice against leading away from tenace holdings. It is true that such a lead can be dangerous but danger is a relative matter. In this case it is much more dangerous not to lead a diamond than to lead one. Any diamond losers that declarer may have are likely to be discarded on dummy's clubs unless you attack at once while you still have trump control.

```
              ♠ K J 8
              ♡ K J 7
              ◇ 6 4
              ♣ A K Q 9 5
♠ A 10 7 6 2         ♠ Q 4 3
♡ A 3                ♡ 10 6 2
◇ K J 9              ◇ Q 8 7 5 3
♣ 8 7 3              ♣ J 6
              ♠ 9 5
              ♡ Q 9 8 5 4
              ◇ A 10 2
              ♣ 10 4 2
```

When declarer wins his ace of diamonds he should, of course, lead a spade. If he sees no danger and plays a trump instead you have got him. Your ace of trumps wins the second round and two further rounds of diamonds lock declarer in dummy with no way back to his hand to draw the last trump. Without the initial diamond lead the defence would have no chance at all.

♠ Q 10 8 4 3
♡ 10 9 5
♢ 7 2
♣ 9 6 4

		E	S	W	N
		1 ♠	—	2 ♠	Dbl.
		3 ♠	4 ♢	—	5 ♢
		All pass			

Dummy is likely to be strong but there is no indication as to which of the unbid suits you ought to lead. If you could lay down an ace and have a look at dummy that might help. You have no ace, unfortunately, but the lead of the queen of spades might serve as well.

♠ 6
♡ K J 7 4
♣ K Q 5 3
♣ A Q J 7

♠ Q 10 8 4 3   ♠ A K 9 5 2
♡ 10 9 5   ♡ 8 3 2
♢ 7 2   ♢ A
♣ 9 6 4   ♣ K 8 5 3

♠ J 7
♡ A Q 6
♢ J 10 9 8 6 4
♣ 10 2

Your partner's two of spades on the first trick will leave you in no doubt as to which suit to switch to. On the orthodox lead of your fourth highest spade the contract would have been impregnable.

Usually it is a good idea to have a look at dummy when the only bid has been pre-emptive.

♠ Q J 6
♡ A Q 8
♢ J 8 5 4 2
♣ 9 7

		N	E	S	W
		—	—	4 ♠	All pass

When this was posed as an opening lead problem in the Swedish magazine *Bridgetidningen* the majority vote of the panel of experts was for the ace of hearts, the queen of spades coming a close second. As it happened, either lead would have served the defence well for the full hand was as follows.

```
            ♠ 2
            ♡ 7 4 3 2
            ◇ A K 9
            ♣ 6 5 4 3 2
♠ Q J 6                      ♠ 10 4
♡ A Q 8        N             ♡ K J 10 5
◇ J 8 5 4 2   W   E          ◇ Q 10 7 6 3
♣ 9 7            S           ♣ K J
            ♠ A K 9 8 7 5 3
            ♡ 9 6
            ◇ —
            ♣ A Q 10 8
```

The defenders still have to exercise a little care. West must
guard against being thrown in to lead a minor suit. If three rounds
of hearts are played immediately South will make his contract.

Another good occasion to start with an ace is against a gambling
three no trumps.

```
♠ A Q 10 6 2   N       N     E     S      W
♡ 9 8 3      W    E     —     —    3 NT   All pass
◇ 5            S
♣ J 9 8 6
```

The best lead here is the ace of spades, although on occasion
it may make life hard for your partner.

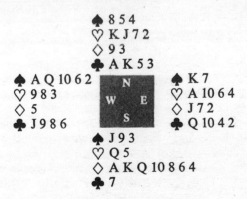

```
            ♠ 8 5 4
            ♡ K J 7 2
            ◇ 9 3
            ♣ A K 5 3
♠ A Q 10 6 2                 ♠ K 7
♡ 9 8 3        N             ♡ A 10 6 4
◇ 5           W   E          ◇ J 7 2
♣ J 9 8 6       S            ♣ Q 10 4 2
            ♠ J 9 3
            ♡ Q 5
            ◇ A K Q 10 8 6 4
            ♣ 7
```

East can see that the spade suit is the only possible source of nourishment for the defence and must unblock by playing his king under the ace. Now a heart to partner's marked ace and a spade return will produce the happy ending.

It is true that an initial heart lead and spade switch will defeat the contract with less cerebration all round, but to lead from a small trebleton against this kind of bidding will be losing tactics in the long run.

Many players do not sufficiently appreciate the need for aggression when leading against a small slam. When the opponents voluntarily contract for twelve tricks they will usually have no shortage of tricks in the combined hands if they are given time to develop them. Don't give them time. Try to develop two tricks for yourself first. If you have a king or a queen in an unbid suit, lead that suit and hope that partner can help. You will not invariably succeed but on balance an aggressive policy will pay.

♠ J 10 9 8 3
♡ Q 7 2
◇ A
♣ K 8 5 2

		S	W
		1 ♣	1 ◇
		2 ♠	4 ♣
		6 ♣	—

No doubt you expect to defeat this contract. Perhaps you even considered doubling. But you must still select your opening lead with care, and the correct lead here is the two of hearts. This risks absolutely nothing, for if you do not lead the suit declarer's heart losers will certainly go away on dummy's diamonds. If you choose the 'safe' spade lead you will regret it, for the full hand is:

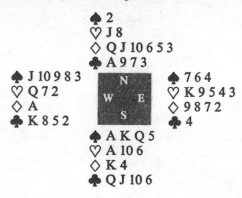

♠ 2
♡ J 8
◇ Q J 10 6 5 3
♣ A 9 7 3

♠ J 10 9 8 3
♡ Q 7 2
◇ A
♣ K 8 5 2

♠ 7 6 4
♡ K 9 5 4 3
◇ 9 8 7 2
♣ 4

♠ A K Q 5
♡ A 10 6
◇ K 4
♣ Q J 10 6

Sometimes you may get a little help from partner in deciding what to lead.

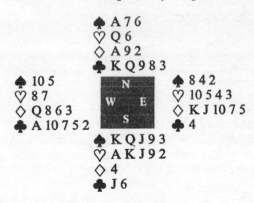

♠ 10 5		S	W	N	E
♡ 8 7		1 ♠	—	2 ♣	—
◇ Q 8 6 3		2 ♡	—	3 ◇	Dbl.
♣ A 10 7 5 2		3 ♡	—	5 ♠	—
		6 ♠	All pass		

Partner doubled the diamond bid to indicate a safe lead and you should be duly grateful to him. Without the double you would probably have led a diamond, but now you certainly should not. East must have some length in the suit to have doubled at the three-level, and it is unlikely that you can take a trick in diamonds. South doesn't think you can, anyway, or he would not have bid the slam. Declarer has shown ten cards in the majors and he may well have a doubleton club. The best chance of defeating this contract is to lead your ace of clubs and follow with a second round in the hope that your partner can ruff.

```
                ♠ A 7 6
                ♡ Q 6
                ◇ A 9 2
                ♣ K Q 9 8 3
  ♠ 10 5                      ♠ 8 4 2
  ♡ 8 7                       ♡ 10 5 4 3
  ◇ Q 8 6 3                   ◇ K J 10 7 5
  ♣ A 10 7 5 2                ♣ 4
                ♠ K Q J 9 3
                ♡ A K J 9 2
                ◇ 4
                ♣ J 6
```

5 • To Love and to Cherish

The time has come to examine in a little more detail the delicate matter of partnership co-operation. In particular we shall have a look at some of the ways in which you can smooth the worried frown from the face across the table and replace it with a grateful smile. After all you are stuck with your partner for the duration of the rubber (or the tournament, as the case may be) and you may as well make the best of it. It is in your own interest to ease your partner's burden in any way you can.

Good defenders show a consideration for each other's problems that is not entirely altruistic. From experience they have absorbed the bitter lesson that all players are apt to err on occasion, but instead of waiting fatalistically for their partner's errors they take active steps to prevent or mitigate them. This is an admirable attitude. It is undoubtedly more charitable to prevent your partner from making mistakes than to point out afterwards exactly where he went wrong and why he should have played differently. It is also much more profitable.

You must acquire the habit of looking at each hand not only from your own point of view but from your partner's angle as well. In selecting a line of play you must ask yourself how your play will affect your partner's hand, his view of the situation, his next lead, his whole defence. You must work out his holding, anticipate his problems, spot the possible mistake before he makes it and try to think up some means of setting him on the right path. You must cherish your partner, wrap him up in cotton wool and protect him from the wiles of the declarer and from his own blunders in so far as you can.

All this brotherly love is not a one-way activity of course; it is reciprocal. While you are looking after your partner he will, or at any rate should, be doing the same for you. It seldom happens that both defenders are equally well-informed during the early stages of the play. One will know more about the hand than the other, perhaps because he can see more of the honour cards, perhaps for some other reason. Frequently it is the partner of the opening leader who is the better informed due to the inferences available from the opening lead. When you know more about the hand than your partner does it is up to you to see that the defence is guided on the right lines. If you can see your way clear to defeating the contract you must try to take charge of the defence rather than leave your partner on lead in a guessing situation. If you are unable to do this and if the standard signals cannot help, you must try to improvise. There will usually be some way of giving partner the information he needs to find the killing defence.

♠ A K 10 3
♡ A Q 6
◇ 9 4
♣ A J 8 2

N	S
1 ♣	1 ◇
2 NT	3 ◇
—	

♠ J 9 5
♡ K J 7
◇ 6 3
♣ K Q 7 6 4

West leads the nine of clubs and the two is played from dummy. How do you plan the defence?

You know that your partner has either a singleton or a doubleton in clubs. Even if he has a singleton there seems little point in returning the suit, for partner would have to ruff a loser with what might well be a natural trump stopper. Partner is marked with some high cards in diamonds on this bidding. The only hope appears to be that you can take, in addition to your club, two trump and two heart tricks. If your partner has another club you do not wish him to lead it when he gets in, for that would very likely be fatal for the defence. The way to make sure he switches to hearts is to win the first trick with the king of clubs, not the queen. Then you can return a diamond and let events take their course.

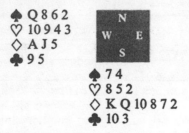

♠ Q 8 6 2
♡ 10 9 4 3
◇ A J 5
♣ 9 5

♠ 7 4
♡ 8 5 2
◇ K Q 10 8 7 2
♣ 10 3

Certainly West should be able to work out for himself that he must switch to hearts even if you had won the first trick with the queen of clubs. But your play of the king made it practically impossible for him to go wrong. Such plays save your partner a lot of mental effort and make the game easier for him, which is worth plenty of points in the long run.

```
                    ♠ Q 9 6
                    ♡ A 8 3
                    ◇ 9 5
                    ♣ A 10 7 3 2
    S       N                       ♠ J 10 8 3
    1♠      2♣      N               ♡ J 6 5
    2♡      3♠    W     E           ◇ J 4 2
    3 NT    —       S               ♣ K J 8
```

Against South's three no trump contract West leads the three of diamonds to your knave and declarer's king. South leads a small heart, your partner puts on the nine and the three is played from dummy. How do you defend?

If you allow your partner to hold this trick he will certainly switch, but will he make the right switch? You know from the opening lead that declarer started with four diamonds and therefore, since he bid both majors, not more than one club, but that information is not available to your partner. Rather than risk your partner taking a wrong view, you must win this trick with your knave of hearts and lead the king of clubs.

```
    ♠ 7 5
    ♡ Q 10 9              N
    ◇ A 10 6 3        W       E
    ♣ 9 6 5 4              S

                    ♠ A K 4 2
                    ♡ K 7 4 2
                    ◇ K Q 8 7
                    ♣ Q
```

If your king of clubs is allowed to hold the trick, a diamond to partner's ten will permit him to lead another club through dummy. Here again partner could probably have found the club switch unaided, but in such situations it is unkind to let partner sweat it out. As soon as you can see the way to set the contract you should take action to share the secret with your partner.

Against South's four spade contract you lead the ace of diamonds and follow with the king, South ruffing the second round. Declarer cashes the king of spades and leads a small spade to dummy's ace. Partner follows with the three and the knave and you throw the four of clubs. The knave of hearts is now led from dummy and allowed to run to your queen. How should you continue?

It looks as though your partner has a third defensive trick in the queen of spades, for South will not have seven spades on this bidding. Where is the setting trick to come from? If partner has either the heart or the club ace he cannot be prevented from making it. Is there any hope if South has both aces? Only if the declarer's shape is 6-4-1-2 and partner has the king of clubs. A club return would not be safe for declarer might have A 10. A diamond looks safe enough, but would in fact be highly dangerous. If you are thinking of your partner's problems you will make the passive return of a heart.

Partner would not thank you for leading a diamond and thus helping declarer to strip him of all his exit cards before throwing him in to lead away from his king of clubs.

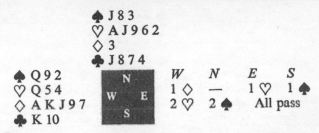

♠ J 8 3
♡ A J 9 6 2
◇ 3
♣ J 8 7 4

♠ Q 9 2
♡ Q 5 4
◇ A K J 9 7
♣ K 10

W	N	E	S
1 ◇	—	1 ♡	1 ♠
2 ♡	2 ♠	All pass	

Against South's two spade contract you lead the ace of diamonds, regretting it when you see dummy. You switch to the two of spades and your partner's king forces South's ace. A heart to the ace is followed by a heart ruff, a diamond ruff, another heart ruff and another diamond ruff, your partner playing the ten on the third round of diamonds. Now declarer leads a club to his ace, on which you drop the king, and leads the queen of diamonds. How do you defend?

The cards remaining in your hand are ♠ Q 9, ◇ K J, ♣ 10, and dummy has ♡ J 9, ♣ J 8 7. Declarer has made seven tricks and clearly cannot be prevented from making his contract if he has all three of the outstanding trumps. You must assume he has only two of them, in which case the play is obvious. Win the king of diamonds, lead the ten of clubs to your partner's queen and either a trump lead or the king of hearts from partner will serve to pick up declarer's trumps.

The trouble with that line of play is that it is not quite foolproof. It is true that a good player should have no doubts about overtaking your ten of clubs when dummy plays low, but there is no need to put your partner to the test. You can force him to defeat the contract by the simple device of playing your knave of diamonds on declarer's queen.

♠ K 4
♡ K 10 8 7
◇ 10 6 5
♣ Q 9 5 2

♠ A 10 7 6 5
♡ 3
◇ Q 8 4 2
♣ A 6 3

```
              ♠ J 8 6
              ♡ K J 9 3
              ◇ K Q J
              ♣ K 10 2
Match-point pairs    N        ♠ Q 9 2
Game all       W         E    ♡ Q 10 5
  N      S           S        ◇ 8 7 5
  1 ♡    1 NT                 ♣ A Q J 9
```

West leads the three of spades against South's contract of one no trump. Dummy plays low, you put in the nine and declarer wins with the king. South now plays on diamonds, overtaking dummy's king on the third round with the ace and leading the ten, on which partner throws the two of hearts and dummy a spade. How do you defend?

Declarer has shown up with seven points already, so partner must have both major suit aces. That means that you can make the rest of the tricks—three spades, the ace of hearts and four clubs if you can persuade partner to lead the suit twice. Partner will have difficulty in believing that your clubs are quite so solid, however, and he may play low on the coming heart lead in the hope that declarer will misguess. The two of hearts might even be taken as an indication that partner intends to play low. To dissuade him from that course and tell him that you have the clubs under complete control you must discard your queen of hearts.

```
♠ A 10 5 3        N
♡ A 7 4 2     W       E
◇ 9 6 2           S
♣ 5 4
                ♠ K 7 4
                ♡ 8 6
                ◇ A 10 4 3
                ♣ 8 7 6 3
```

Declarer could have given himself a better chance of stealing a sixth trick by leading a heart at trick two.

♠ 9 4
♡ K J 6
♢ A 8 7 3 2
♣ K 10 3

S	N		♠ Q J 2
1 ♣	1 ♢		♡ Q 8 6 4 2
1 NT[1]	3 NT		♢ Q 10 6 4
—			♣ 5

West leads the seven of spades against South's three no trump contract and your knave is captured by declarer's king. A small club is led to dummy's king and the ten of clubs returned. How do you defend?

It may well be that your partner has a club stopper, but when he gets in he will be uncertain how to continue. From his side of the table it may be hard to tell whether he should carry on with spades or switch to one of the red suits in the hope of finding your entry so that you can lead through declarer's presumed queen of spades.

It is your duty to prevent your partner from going wrong. You know from the Rule of Eleven that declarer has no more spades higher than the seven, and you must give your partner the glad news by discarding your spade queen.

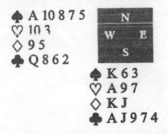

♠ A 10 8 7 5
♡ 10 3
♢ 9 5
♣ Q 8 6 2

♠ K 6 3
♡ A 9 7
♢ K J
♣ A J 9 7 4

Without your help partner might play for you to have the king of diamonds and a heart stopper and make a fatal switch.

Situations where the defence have to cash their top tricks before declarer can get in are quite common. Both defenders must keep on the alert for subtle inferences and must take care not to mislead each other in the information they exchange.

[1] 15–16 points.

♠ A Q J 7
♡ 8 4
◇ K 9 6 2
♣ 10 9 5

W	N	E	S
—	—	1 ♡	3 ♣
—	4 ♣	—	5 ♣
All pass			

♠ 10 8 5
♡ K Q J 7 3
◇ A 10 7 4
♣ 2

Against South's five club contract your partner leads the two of hearts and your knave is taken by declarer's ace. A spade lead from South is won by dummy's knave and the ten of clubs is allowed to run to your partner's king. West now leads the queen of diamonds and the two is played from dummy. How do you defend?

Why do you think your partner switched to diamonds? Obviously it is because he realizes you must have the ace of diamonds to defeat this contract and he is not sure whether a heart trick can be cashed or not. But *you* are sure, for your partner's opening lead of the two of hearts told you that declarer has one more card in the suit. South will have to have one diamond, but you need not gamble on his having two. It is your clear duty to play the ace of diamonds on your partner's queen and cash the king of hearts.

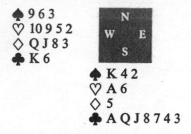

♠ 9 6 3
♡ 10 9 5 2
◇ Q J 8 3
♣ K 6

♠ K 4 2
♡ A 6
◇ 5
♣ A Q J 8 7 4 3

South could have made his contract by cashing his ace of clubs at trick two and following with four rounds of spades. As the play went, if you had played low on the queen of diamonds your partner would have assumed you started with six hearts and would have tried for the setting trick in diamonds.

♠ 10 4
♡ Q 8 2
◇ A Q J 5
♣ Q 8 5 4

♠ Q J 8 7 5 2
♡ A 7 4
◇ 8 6 3
♣ 7

S	N
1♣	3♣
5♣	—

Your partner leads the five of hearts against South's five club contract and you win with the ace, declarer following with the six. How should you continue?

On this bidding South is marked with at least six and probably seven clubs. Dummy's diamond holding is very discouraging. If declarer has the ace of spades as well he is certain to make his contract. Since you have to play for your partner to have the ace of spades it might seem a good plan to lead the spade queen at trick two in an attempt to trap South's king. But that play would be a grave dereliction of duty. You do not require two spade tricks to defeat this contract; one will suffice. Partner does not know that declarer has another heart, but you do and you must make this clear by returning the seven of hearts at trick two. Then partner can cash his ace of spades for the setting trick.

♠ A 9 6 3
♡ K J 9 5 3
◇ 10 7 2
♣ 9

♠ K
♡ 10 6
◇ K 9 4
♣ A K J 10 6 3 2

Had you made the irresponsible return of the queen of spades your partner would have inferred that you had four hearts and would have tried to give you the setting trick in spades.

♠ J 6
♥ J 7 5 4
♦ K Q 3 2
♣ A K Q

♠ A Q
♥ K Q 10 6
♦ 10 7
♣ J 8 7 4 2

N	S
1 ♦	1 ♠
1 NT	3 ♠
4 ♠	—

You lead the king of hearts against South's four spade contract, your partner following with the nine and declarer with the two. How should you continue?

What can South have for his bidding? Clearly the ace of diamonds and six or seven spades headed by the king. Then there are just two possible ways in which you might defeat this contract. You can try to cash another heart trick, or you can play for your partner to have three trumps and a doubleton club and try to give him a third round club ruff. Which do you choose?

The clue is your partner's play of the nine of hearts. In situations of this kind the echo should be used to show distribution. The presence of the heart knave in dummy makes it unnecessary for your partner to show his ace. He knows that when your king of hearts holds the trick you will not be in doubt as to the location of the ace, and with only three hearts he would have played low. So partner is showing four hearts, in which case your only chance is to lead a club at trick two.

♠ 7 4 3
♥ A 9 8 3
♦ J 9 8 5
♣ 6 5

♠ K 10 9 8 5 2
♥ 2
♦ A 6 4
♣ 10 9 3

♠ A 6
♡ K Q 10 9 6 2
◇ K
♣ A 7 5 3

N–S Game

W	N	E	S
1 ◇	Dbl.	1 ♠	2 ♡
4 ♠	5 ♡	All pass	

♠ K 9 7 5 2
♡ 8 5 4
◇ 8
♣ Q 10 9 8

West leads the queen of spades against South's five heart contract and you drop the nine under dummy's ace. Three rounds of trumps are played, on which your partner discards the five, two and three of diamonds. The king of diamonds is led from dummy, South playing the seven and your partner winning with the ace. West now leads the knave of spades. How do you defend?

If South is going to ruff this trick there is nothing you can do to influence the result of the contract. But if South has another spade the contract will be defeated if you can make just one club trick. You can see that a club lead from either side cannot give away a trick, but if partner has something like knave and another a club lead may look very dangerous to him. To prevent your partner from going wrong you must play your king on his knave of spades and lead a club.

♠ Q J 10 3
♡ —
◇ A Q 9 5 4 3 2
♣ J 4

♠ 8 4
♡ A J 7 3
◇ J 10 7 6
♣ K 6 2

If you allow your partner's knave of spades to hold the trick he may be misled by declarer's false card in diamonds. Putting declarer with four clubs, he will switch to diamonds with fatal results.

```
                    ♠ 4
                    ♡ A 10 6
                    ◇ K Q 9 8 5 2
                    ♣ K 9 3
    ♠ A Q 8 7 5 3       N         N    E    S    W
    ♡ K 8 4                       1◇   —    1♡   1♠
    ◇ J 7          W       E      2♡   3♠   4♡   —
    ♣ Q 6             S           —    4♠   5♡   Dbl.
                              All pass
```

With no very attractive lead, you try the knave of diamonds against South's doubled contract of five hearts. The king is played from dummy and East wins with the ace while South plays the six. Your partner now switches to the knave of spades and declarer follows with the two. How do you plan the defence?

You will probably say that this one is too easy. You can see that, as long as South has another spade, the contract can be defeated by forcing dummy to ruff and thus making sure of a trump trick for yourself. *You* can see this but your partner cannot. The point is that you must do it yourself by overtaking partner's knave with your queen and continuing with the ace. You must on no account adopt the half measure of playing your eight of spades under your partner's knave. If you leave East on play at this point nothing in this world is more certain than that he will switch back to diamonds.

```
              N         ♠ K J 10 6
          W       E      ♡ —
              S          ◇ A 10 4 3
                         ♣ J 10 8 4 2
    ♠ 9 2
    ♡ Q J 9 7 5 3 2
    ◇ 6
    ♣ A 7 5
```

Even if you were missing the queen of spades it would still be correct play to overtake partner's knave with your ace and return a small one.

```
                  ♠ J 10 7
                  ♡ 10 6 4
                  ◇ A K Q 10 3
                  ♣ 9 4
   S     N                        ♠ 6 5 3
   1 ♠   2 ◇                      ♡ K 8 5
   2 ♠   3 ♠                      ◇ J 6
   4 ♠   —                        ♣ J 8 7 5 2
```

West leads the three of clubs against South's four spade contract. How do you plan the defence?

There can be no club tricks for the defence on this hand, for West would not underlead an ace on this bidding, nor would he lead small from the king and queen. Dummy's diamond suit looks dangerous. Clearly the only hope is that partner has a trump trick and that you can make three tricks in hearts. Since you cannot make any tricks in clubs there is no point in making the orthodox third hand high play. In fact it would be a serious blunder to play your club knave. You want your partner to switch to hearts when he gets in, and it is your duty to tell him so in the most unmistakable way by playing your two of clubs to the first trick.

You might think it can make little difference whether you play the two or the knave. That the difference can be vital is shown by what happened when the hand was played.

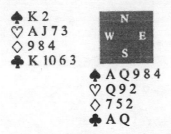

```
   ♠ K 2
   ♡ A J 7 3
   ◇ 9 8 4
   ♣ K 10 6 3

                  ♠ A Q 9 8 4
                  ♡ Q 9 2
                  ◇ 7 5 2
                  ♣ A Q
```

East put up the club knave and South won with the ace! After a diamond to the ace and a losing spade finesse, West naturally tried to put his partner in with the club queen to lead hearts through, and the declarer made eleven tricks.

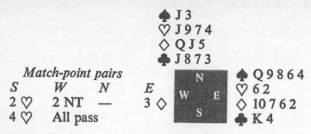

Match-point pairs

S	W	N	E
2 ♡	2 NT	—	3 ◇
4 ♡	All pass		

♠ J 3
♡ J 9 7 4
◇ Q J 5
♣ J 8 7 3

♠ Q 9 8 6 4
♡ 6 2
◇ 10 7 6 2
♣ K 4

West leads the ten of spades and the knave is played from dummy. How do you plan the defence?

On the bidding your partner is marked with at least ten cards in the minor suits. He could have two spades and one heart or, more likely, three spades. In either case it is clear that declarer will make his contract for he can ruff his spade losers in dummy. Then you must limit your ambition to making all the tricks you are entitled to in the minor suits. As always, the best way of making sure partner switches when he gets in again is to play low. There is no point whatsoever in covering the spade knave with your queen. If you do and declarer wins with the ace partner will be left in doubt as to who has the king. Don't leave him in doubt. Play the four of spades on the first trick.

♠ 10 7 2
♡ —
◇ A 9 8 4 3
♣ A Q 10 6 2

♠ A K 5
♡ A K Q 10 8 5 3
◇ K
♣ 9 5

Even if you play the queen of spades at trick one you will have another chance of helping partner. When declarer crosses to dummy with a trump and leads the five of diamonds, your two should tell partner which suit to lead. But there is nothing like making doubly sure.

6 · A Further Count

I make no apology for returning in this chapter to hammer away at the same old theme. Good habits are formed by constant repetition, and it is only by working through a large number of problems of this sort that the reader can hope to acquire the most valuable of all bridge habits. The defender who makes a real effort to construct a blueprint of the hidden hands on every deal enjoys an overwhelming advantage in play.

The problems in this chapter have the familiar common factor. Counting and logical inference are the twin keys to successful defence.

```
              ♠ A Q 6
              ♡ 9 4 3 2
              ◇ 9 5 3
              ♣ Q 10 7

♠ 8 2                          S    W     N     E
♡ A K Q 6                      1 ♠  Dbl.  1 NT  —
◇ A 10 7 6                     2 ♣  —     3 ♠   —
♣ 9 3 2                        4 ♠  All pass
```

You lead the ace of hearts against South's four spade contract,
your partner playing the seven and declarer the five. How should
you continue?

With five spades and five clubs it is usual to bid the minor suit
first, so South probably has only four clubs. If he has no losers
in spades or clubs, as appears likely, he will have nine top tricks,
and you will have to win four tricks for the defence in the red
suits. However, this seems to be one of those hands in which
declarer's losers cannot run away and in such cases it is almost
always best to defend passively.

At present you cannot tell whether declarer has one heart and
three diamonds or two of each suit, and it may seem safe enough
to continue with a second round of hearts to find out. In fact it
is far from safe. If declarer has no more hearts he may then have
enough entries to ruff out all dummy's hearts and make his contract by dummy reversal. A trump lead at trick two is your
safest play.

```
                        ♠ 9 5 3
                        ♡ J 10 8 7
                        ◇ Q J 4
                        ♣ 8 6 5

              ♠ K J 10 7 4
              ♡ 5
              ◇ K 8 2
              ♣ A K J 4
```

♠ 9 5
♥ K 6 4
♦ K J 8 7
♣ Q J 10 6

S	N
1 ♣	3 ♣
3 NT	—

♠ J 6 4 3 2
♥ Q J 9 3
♦ 10 5 4
♣ 2

West leads the seven of spades and the nine is played from dummy. How do you plan the defence?

Your partner's seven is probably a fourth-highest lead, in which case declarer can have no more than two spades. It seems certain that partner will have an outside entry and the defence may be able to take four spade tricks to defeat the contract. Unfortunately there is a snag. If you cover dummy's nine of spades with your knave you will have no card left that is high enough to take over the lead from your partner in order to cash the fifth spade. Could it help to play low on this trick, or might that be too expensive? It would certainly cost a trick if partner has led from the king and queen and declarer is allowed to win with his ten. If that is the case the spade suit is blocked and will only yield three tricks if you put up your knave. Partner would then need two outside tricks to defeat the contract. But if partner has two outside tricks (they can only be the ace of diamonds and one of the top clubs) you will defeat the contract even if you play low. Declarer will be unable to muster nine tricks before the defence takes five. You should therefore play the six of spades to the first trick.

♠ A 10 8 7
♥ 10 7 2
♦ Q 6 3
♣ K 8 5

♠ K Q
♥ A 8 5
♦ A 9 2
♣ A 9 7 4 3

♠ J 8 3
♡ Q J 10
◇ 8 4
♣ A K J 10 2

♠ Q 10 9 4
♡ K 8 7
◇ A K Q 9 5
♣ 3

N	E	S	W
1 ♣	—	1 ♠	2 ◇
—	—	3 ◇	—
3 ♠	—	4 ♣	All pass

You lead the ace of diamonds against South's four spade contract, your partner following with the two and declarer with the
three. It doesn't look as though you can put partner in to give
you a club ruff, so you continue with two further rounds of diamonds, dummy ruffing the third round while partner and declarer
follow suit. South now enters his hand with the queen of clubs
and leads the five of spades. How do you plan the defence?

Declarer presumably has a five-card trump suit headed by ace
and king, and he is marked with the ace of hearts. It will not help
to play low on this trick, for after winning with dummy's knave
South would continue with three more rounds of trumps, thus
losing only two diamonds and a trump trick. Nor will it do any
good to win the queen of spades and continue diamonds. South
would ruff in hand, cross to the knave of spades, return with the
ace of hearts and draw the outstanding trumps. The only way to
win a fourth defensive trick is to block trumps and attack the
entry to declarer's hand. Provided that declarer has not less than
three hearts, you can defeat this contract for certain by winning
the queen of spades and returning the king of hearts.

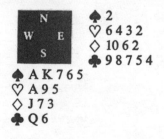

♠ 2
♡ 6 4 3 2
◇ 10 6 2
♣ 9 8 7 5 4

♠ A K 7 6 5
♡ A 9 5
◇ J 7 3
♣ Q 6

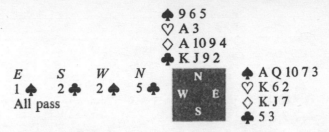

```
            ♠ 9 6 5
            ♡ A 3
            ◇ A 10 9 4
            ♣ K J 9 2
E    S    W    N                      ♠ A Q 10 7 3
1♠   2♣   2♠   5♣                     ♡ K 6 2
All pass                             ◇ K J 7
                                     ♣ 5 3
```

West leads the two of spades against South's five club contract.
You win the ace and continue with a second spade, which declarer ruffs. A trump is played to the king, dummy's third spade
is ruffed and a second round of trumps won by South's ace, your
partner discarding the king of spades. Declarer now leads the
queen of diamonds and runs it to your king. How do you continue?

If you have been counting you will realize that you can defeat
this contract for certain. Declarer has shown up with six clubs
and a singleton spade. He has therefore six cards in the red suits
and cannot get rid of his heart loser unless you help him. A spade
return will be all the help he needs if his shape is 1-4-2-6. He will
ruff in hand and throw the small heart from dummy and ruff out
your knave of diamonds to make dummy good. A heart return
runs the obvious risk of declarer having the queen, therefore by a
process of elimination you are left with the diamond suit. A
recount shows that a diamond return is perfectly safe. Declarer is
welcome to three diamonds, six clubs and the ace of hearts, for
that adds up to only ten tricks.

```
♠ K J 8 2
♡ J 10 7 4
◇ 8 6 5 3
♣ 6
                    ♠ 4
                    ♡ Q 9 8 5
                    ◇ Q 2
                    ♣ A Q 10 8 7 4
```

```
        ♠ A Q 7 2
        ♡ J 10 4
        ◇ J 8 7
        ♣ A Q 3
♠ J 10 6                         N      S
♡ A 8 2          N              1 ♠    2 NT
◇ Q 5 2       W     E           3 NT    —
♣ J 9 7 4         S
```

With no very attractive lead against South's three no trump contract, you try the knave of spades. The two is played from dummy, partner plays the three and the declarer wins with the king. South now leads the three of hearts. How do you plan the defence?

What is South's heart holding likely to be? He could have the king and queen in which case it would seem that the only hope for the defence is to take four tricks in diamonds. Perhaps more likely is that declarer's four hearts are headed by the queen. Then in addition to your two heart tricks you will have to develop three tricks in one of the minor suits, which means playing for partner to have king and ten in that suit. Which of the minors do you fancy? If you are going to attack clubs it will have to be done from your side of the table. The trouble is that if you go up with your ace of hearts to lead a club the declarer can hold up and block the suit, and you will never make your long club for lack of an entry. Prospects are better in diamonds, for you are in a position to see to it that the entry in the long diamond hand is not knocked out too early. The conclusion is that your proper play, whatever declarer may hold, is to take your ace of hearts immediately and lead the two of diamonds.

```
                      ♠ 8 5 3
            N         ♡ K 6 5
         W     E      ◇ K 10 6 4
            S         ♣ 10 8 2
        ♠ K 9 4
        ♡ Q 9 7 3
        ◇ A 9 3
        ♣ K 6 5
```

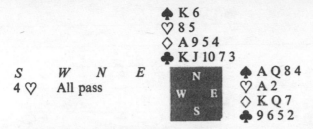

♠ K 6
♡ 8 5
◇ A 9 5 4
♣ K J 10 7 3

S	W	N	E
4 ♡	All pass		

♠ A Q 8 4
♡ A 2
◇ K Q 7
♣ 9 6 5 2

West leads the two of spades, the king is played from dummy and your ace wins. How do you plan the defence?

The opening lead has told you that declarer has three spades. Also, your partner will have the knave of spades, for it is a fairly safe inference that South would not have played dummy's king if he had the knave in his hand. South must have at least seven trumps for his pre-emptive bid, and therefore not more than three cards in the minor suits. If your partner has the ace of clubs the contract is likely to be defeated, but if declarer has that card you will have to defend with care. There is no hope if South has the ace of clubs and eight or more trumps, so assume he has only seven. A diamond return at trick two will serve well enough if declarer has a doubleton diamond and singleton ace of clubs, but if he has a singleton diamond the diamond switch will lose a vital tempo. There is no point in leading a club, for with a weak hand partner would have led a singleton if he had one. The defence that will always succeed if your partner has two hearts is to switch to the two of hearts at trick two.

♠ J 9 5 2
♡ 7 4
◇ J 10 8 6 3
♣ Q 8

♠ 10 7 3
♡ K Q J 10 9 6 3
◇ 2
♣ A 4

The underlead of the ace of trumps retains control and ensures three spade tricks or two spades and a club ruff for the defence.

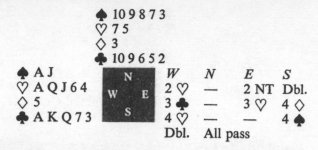

	W	N	E	S
	2 ♡	—	2 NT	Dbl.
	3 ♣	—	3 ♡	4 ◇
	4 ♡	—	—	4 ♠
	Dbl.	All pass		

Annoyed at being outbid on your big hand, you double South's four spade call and lead the ace of clubs. When you see dummy you begin to regret your double. On the first trick your partner plays the eight and declarer the knave. How do you plan the defence?

Partner's eight is probably the start of an echo and declarer's knave a true card. For the moment there is nothing better to do than continue clubs, but you should continue by leading the queen. If by any chance your partner's eight of clubs *was* a singleton you would like him to ruff this trick and play a heart through. But no, partner follows with the four and declarer ruffs. The king of spades is led and you win, partner following with the two. To try everything in the proper order you should next cash the ace of hearts and see what that produces. Disappointment! Partner plays the three and declarer the two. Unlikely as it may be, the only remaining hope is that your partner has the six of spades and can use it to promote your knave. You lead the three of clubs and your perseverance is rewarded when the other hands turn out to be:

♠ K965
♡ AJ4
◇ KQJ3
♣ 86

N	*S*
1 NT	3 ♡
4 ♡	—

♠ A873
♡ K72
◇ 108764
♣ A

West leads the knave of clubs against South's four heart contract and you get off to a faultless start by winning with the ace. How should you continue?

Once again this is a matter of counting your own tricks. At the moment you can see three—a club, a spade and a trump. Where is the setting trick to come from? It is no use hoping for a spade lead through dummy. Even if your partner has queen and knave he will never get in to lead through, and when the declarer has drawn trumps his spade losers will be discarded on dummy's diamonds. Since there is no chance of a second spade trick the fourth defensive trick will have to be a club ruff, and to engineer a club ruff you must find an entry in partner's hand. At first sight this may appear hopeless, but there is one possibility. If declarer has a doubleton spade and your partner's spades are as good as Q 10 x, you will be able to create an entry in your partner's hand by underleading your ace twice. Your partner will also need to have two trumps to prevent the immediate run of the diamonds. As the only hope, then, you should lead the three of spades at trick two.

♠ Q 10 4
♡ 6 5
◇ 9 5
♣ J 10 9 7 4 2

♠ J 2
♡ Q 10 9 8 3
◇ A 2
♣ K Q 5 3

♠ A J 9 6 3
♡ 7
♢ A K Q 8
♣ 7 6 3

♠ 7 4
♡ Q J 10 8
♢ J 7 6 3
♣ A Q J

	N	S
	1 ♠	2 ♡
	2 ♠	3 ♣
	3 ♢	3 NT

You lead the queen of hearts against South's three no trump contract, your partner plays the five and the declarer wins with the ace. The queen of spades is now led, dummy plays low and your partner wins with the king. East returns the eight of clubs which is covered by declarer's nine and won by your knave. How should you continue?

On the bidding South can hardly have more than a doubleton spade, therefore your partner started with four. The key card is the ten of spades. Who is likely to have it? There is, in fact, a strong indication that declarer has the ten. With a second spade stopper your partner would probably have returned a heart to set up some tricks for you in that suit. He has switched to clubs because he can see that declarer's spades are solid and knows that the king of hearts will be South's ninth trick.

Is there any way of preventing declarer from making his contract? The only hope is that he has a singleton diamond. If so, a diamond lead from you will sever his communications and make it impossible for him to run dummy's spade suit *and* score his king of hearts. There is one further point. To guard against the possibility of declarer's singleton being the ten you must lead the knave of diamonds.

♠ K 8 5 2
♡ 6 5
♢ 9 5 4 2
♣ 8 5 2

♠ Q 10
♡ A K 9 4 3 2
♢ 10
♣ K 10 9 4

```
              ♠ Q 10 9 3
              ♡ 9 4 3
              ◇ Q 7
              ♣ K 8 7 2
♠ 6 2                              S      N
♡ K J 10 7 6 2                     1 ♠    2 ♠
◇ 9 3                              4 ♣    —
♣ Q J 10
```

Against South's four spade contract you lead the queen of clubs, which is allowed to hold the trick. You continue with the knave and then the ten of clubs and declarer ruffs the third round. The ace of spades is cashed and a small spade led to dummy's queen, your partner following suit. The queen of diamonds is covered by the king and ace, the knave of diamonds cashed and a diamond ruffed in dummy, South scowling when you show out. The king of clubs is covered by partner's ace and ruffed by declarer, who now leads the eight of hearts. How do you play to this trick?

Have you been counting? Then you will know that declarer started with five spades, two clubs and at least three diamonds. The bidding marks him with the ace of hearts and if he has only two hearts altogether he is bound to make ten tricks. You must assume, therefore, that declarer has three hearts and partner a singleton. If that singleton is a small card you are not going to defeat this contract, for you will have to return a heart into South's major tenace. To give you any chance East's singleton must be the queen. But you dare not let him win a trick with it, for he would have to return a diamond and give declarer a ruff and discard. Your proper play is to go up with your king of hearts in the hope of dropping partner's queen.

```
                        ♠ 8 5
                        ♡ Q
                        ◇ K 10 8 6 5 2
                        ♣ A 9 6 3
        ♠ A K J 7 4
        ♡ A 8 5
        ◇ A J 4
        ♣ 5 4
```

South was annoyed when you showed out of diamonds because he realized he had misplayed the hand. He should have won the first trump in dummy and led a heart to his ace, then a second trump to dummy followed by the diamond finesse. When you showed out on the third round of diamonds, giving him a complete count of the hand, he would then have been in a position to play the king of clubs and discard a heart on East's ace, whereupon the forced diamond return would have given him a ruff and discard for his contract.

After this misplay the declarer made a good attempt at recovery. He would have succeeded if you had not been counting too.

7 • The Tangled Web

O what a tangled web we weave,
When first we practise to deceive.

Sir Walter Scott, of course, was born a century and a half too
early for bridge. Historians will not even allow that the above
lines might have been inspired by the bitter memory of an un-
successful false card during a game of long whist in the great hall
of Abbotsford. Nevertheless the quotation is apposite enough to
present-day bridge. Few defenders have not experienced at one
time or another the helpless sensation of being enmeshed in a
web of partner's making.

False-carding is an art that requires a delicate touch. It must
never be allowed to become a habit. A good rule to follow is
never to play a false card without a definite purpose in mind. Too
many defenders do the opposite, selecting the cards they play
almost at random, seeking to create confusion for confusion's
sake. An occasional success encourages them in their folly and

enables them to forget the numerous disasters that occur. It is fitting that the first hand in this chapter should tell a cautionary tale.

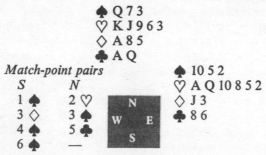

♠ Q 7 3
♡ K J 9 6 3
◇ A 8 5
♣ A Q

Match-point pairs

S	N
1 ♠	2 ♡
3 ◇	3 ♠
4 ♠	5 ♣
6 ♠	—

♠ 10 5 2
♡ A Q 10 8 5 2
◇ J 3
♣ 8 6

West led the four of hearts and the knave was played from dummy. East recognized the lead as a singleton and, seeing no hope of a setting trick elsewhere, decided to try to lull the declarer into a false sense of security by winning with the ace of hearts and returning the five. This plan was not a success as a study of the other two hands will show.

♠ 9
♡ 7 4
◇ 10 9 6 2
♣ J 9 7 5 3 2

♠ A K J 8 6 4
♡ —
◇ K Q 7 4
♣ K 10 4

It is hard to say which defender received the greater shock when South ruffed the ace of hearts. In any case the result was a bottom score for East-West since no other declarer made thirteen tricks.

This is an instructive example of good and bad false-carding on the same trick. East's ace of hearts was a thoughtful and purposeful play that might well have deceived the declarer, whereas West's lead of the lower card from a doubleton was pointless and succeeded only in trapping his partner.

That is the usual fate of aimless false-carding. The reason is not hard to see. The defenders, because of their ignorance of the distribution and total strength of their resources, have to lean heavily on the information they obtain from conventional leads and signals. Declarer, too, can on occasion make profitable use of information conveyed in this manner, but on balance such information is of much greater value to the defenders. It follows, therefore, that any wanton deviation from the conventional in leading or signalling is more likely to deceive your partner than the declarer.

One occasion when it will pay to false-card freely is when you are defending with a weak partner against a strong declarer. Since your partner will rarely notice which card you play it is an ideal time to cut loose with fancy leads in the hope of giving declarer a false picture. When your partner is strong and declarer weak, on the other hand, to indulge in false-carding would be to throw away part of your natural advantage.

Most of the time partner and declarer will be roughly equal in standard. Except in rare cases you should then stick to the rule of giving partner honest information, trusting that it will be of more use to him than to declarer.

You will no doubt be familiar with the mandatory false cards, the situations where you must false-card in order to provide declarer with an alternative to the winning line of play. These have been well covered in numerous textbooks on play and need not be set out here. Nor are we going to discuss the many ducking positions that are deceptive in nature. In this chapter we shall concern ourselves not so much with deceptive plays in a single suit as with the strategic bluffs that are aimed at persuading declarer to miscount.

When you are contemplating playing a false card you should first apply this twofold test:

(1) Is there a real purpose behind the play?

(2) Will it matter if partner is deceived?

If you answer 'yes' to question 1 and 'no' to question 2 you can go ahead with an easy mind.

Consider this hand.

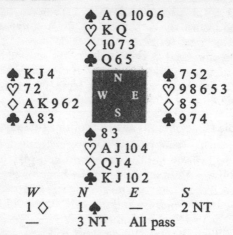

```
                    ♠ A Q 10 9 6
                    ♡ K Q
                    ◇ 10 7 3
                    ♣ Q 6 5
  ♠ K J 4                           ♠ 7 5 2
  ♡ 7 2            N                ♡ 9 8 6 5 3
  ◇ A K 9 6 2    W   E              ◇ 8 5
  ♣ A 8 3            S              ♣ 9 7 4
                    ♠ 8 3
                    ♡ A J 10 4
                    ◇ Q J 4
                    ♣ K J 10 2
```

W	N	E	S
1 ◇	1 ♠	—	2 NT
—	3 NT	All pass	

If West makes the normal lead of the six of diamonds the declarer will probably read the position correctly. When the two of diamonds fails to appear on the first trick he will judge that West has led from a five card suit and that it is therefore unsafe to open up the clubs. His only alternative will be to play for the lucky spade position which in fact exists.

West should realize that this is an ideal opportunity for a deceptive fifth-highest lead of the diamond two. From the bidding he is aware of the menace of the spade suit in dummy, so there is a very real purpose in playing a false card here—to persuade declarer to play on clubs rather than spades. As for partner, the lead may well deceive him but, since the bidding practically marks him with a yarborough, it is certain that partner's play will not affect the outcome of the hand. On such occasions partners ask for nothing better than to be deceived.

For the next hand, which is of a similar type, let us revert to the problem form.

♠ K Q 10 4
♡ A Q 3
◇ 9 6 5
♣ 10 9 7

♠ A 7 5
♡ J 9 7
◇ 8 2
♣ K 8 5 3 2

S	N
1 ◇	1 ♠
1 NT¹	3 NT

You lead the three of clubs against South's three no trump contract. East wins with the ace and returns the six, South playing the four and the knave. How do you plan the defence?

At first glance this looks straightforward enough. Win the king and return the eight to indicate to partner where your entry lies. That would be very superficial reasoning, however. In the first place partner is unlikely to get in again, and secondly there is nothing he could lead but spades if he does. If you remember the bidding you will see that there is a danger that declarer may make his contract without touching spades. Presumably he has the king of hearts, and with three hearts and one club in the bag he will need five tricks from diamonds. Most of his points are in diamonds, he may well have a five card suit, and you can see that any finesse he has to take is right for him. What you have to find is some play that will persuade declarer to play on spades rather than diamonds. You should play the five of clubs on the second trick to make it look as though you started with only four clubs.

♠ 9 8 6 2
♡ 10 6 5 4
◇ Q 7 3
♣ A 6

♠ J 3
♡ K 8 2
◇ A K J 10 4
♣ Q J 4

Observe that once again the false card passes the two fold test. It has a definite purpose, and the fact that partner is deceived is immaterial.

¹ 15–16 points.

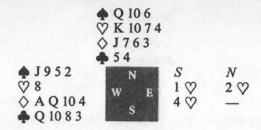

♠ Q 10 6
♡ K 10 7 4
◇ J 7 6 3
♣ 5 4

♠ J 9 5 2
♡ 8
◇ A Q 10 4
♣ Q 10 8 3

	S	N
	1 ♡	2 ♡
	4 ♡	—

You lead the two of spades against South's four heart contract
and your partner wins with the ace. He returns the eight of diamonds, South plays small and your queen wins. You cash the
ace of diamonds on which East plays the nine and South the king.
Then you exit with a spade to declarer's king. South now plays off
the ace and king of clubs and continues with the two of clubs.
How do you play?

The first question to ask yourself is why declarer is playing
clubs instead of trumps. There can be only one answer. He is
trying to count the hand. Presumably he is missing the queen of
trumps and is looking to the fall of the cards in the other suits to
give him a clue to the trump distribution. He knows you have
four spades and four diamonds, and if he suspects you may also
have four clubs he is likely to finesse trumps through your partner's queen. You must try to persuade him to play for the drop
in trumps by playing your queen of clubs to this trick.

♠ A 8 7 4
♡ Q 9 3
◇ 9 8 2
♣ 9 7 6

♠ K 3
♡ A J 6 5 2
◇ K 5
♣ A K J 2

You have to be a fast thinker in such situations. The false card
must be played smoothly and without delay if declarer is to be
taken in.

♠ A Q 3
♡ J 4
◇ Q J 10 9 7 3
♣ K 6

N	S
1 ◇	1 ♡
2 ◇	2 NT
3 NT	

♠ J 10 5
♡ K 7 6 2
◇ A 6
♣ A 10 3 2

West leads the five of clubs, the king is played from dummy and South drops the four on your ace. How should you continue?

What do you think South has in clubs? If your partner's lead is a normal fourth-highest it is fairly certain that declarer has the queen, for with J x x he would not have played the king from dummy. That means that you can establish three club tricks only —not enough to defeat the contract. The only suit that is likely to provide the setting trick is hearts. Partner could have the queen, and if he could make one trick in hearts and then switch back to clubs that would be fine. Should you lead a heart now? The trouble is that declarer is unlikely to co-operate in your plan. He will go up with the ace of hearts and play on diamonds, thus making nine tricks before you can make five.

On this hand you must play on declarer's fear of a five-three club break by continuing with the ten of clubs at trick two. If your ten is allowed to hold you can *now* switch to the seven of hearts and declarer will be unable to play the ace without setting up five tricks for the defence. When partner's queen takes the trick he will reflect on the missing two and three of clubs and probably reach the right conclusion.

♠ 8 7 4 2
♡ Q 8 3
◇ 8 2
♣ J 9 7 5

♠ K 9 6
♡ A 10 9 5
◇ K 5 4
♣ Q 8 4

♠ A 4
♡ 7 4
◇ A Q J 8 6 5
♣ K 7 2

Match-point pairs
S   N
1 NT¹   3 NT

♠ J 8 7 3
♡ K 8 2
◇ K 4
♣ J 9 5 4

Your partner leads the queen of hearts against South's contract of three no trumps. How do you plan the defence?

With such a strong dummy there doesn't appear to be much hope for the defence. You look like making exactly three tricks, for declarer will hold up his ace of hearts until the third round before taking the diamond finesse. Is there any way of making him change his mind?

This time you have to play on declarer's awareness of the desirability of making overtricks at match-point scoring. You should overtake your partner's queen with your king and return the two of hearts. If declarer believes that you have an even number of hearts he will think it safe to play his ace on the second round in order to make sure of the maximum number of tricks if the diamond finesse is right. And if declarer is not deceived you have lost nothing.

♠ 10 6 5
♡ Q J 9 5 3
◇ 10 2
♣ Q 8 3

♠ K Q 9 2
♡ A 10 6
◇ 9 7 3
♣ A 10 6

This hand and the previous one are complementary. In one you try to persuade declarer that you have only three cards in the danger suit, in the other that you have two or four. Opportunities for this type of deceptive play are more common than is generally realized.

¹ 12–14 points.

```
            ♠ 7 5 4
            ♡ A 6
            ◇ K J 8 3
            ♣ Q J 9 2
♠ Q J 10 9                      S        N
♡ 9 5 3                         1 ♡      2 ♣
◇ Q 4                           2 ◇      3 ◇
♣ A K 7 4                       3 NT     —
```

You lead the queen of spades against South's three no trump contract, your partner plays the six and South wins with the king. A small club is now led. Since it would be dangerous to duck you go up with the king and continue with the knave of spades, on which East plays the two and South the ace. Another club is now led. How do you plan your defence?

It is fairly certain that declarer has the ace of diamonds. If he is lacking the ten he can hardly go wrong, but if he has a two-way finesse there is a 50 per cent chance that he will take it into your hand. Can you see any way of increasing that chance to more than 50 per cent?

At this point you should be thankful that you refrained from contesting during the bidding, for declarer does not know you have four spades. You should win the ace of clubs, cash the ten of spades but not the nine, and exit with a club. If declarer is persuaded that you started with only three spades he will think it safe to finesse diamonds into your hand.

```
                           ♠ 8 6 3 2
                           ♡ Q J 8 2
                           ◇ 9 7 5
                           ♣ 6 5
            ♠ A K
            ♡ K 10 7 4
            ◇ A 10 6 2
            ♣ 10 8 3
```

No false card was required here, but unobtrusive deceptive moves like this can be very effective.

```
              ♠ Q 7 5 2
              ♡ A Q 10 6
              ◇ 9
              ♣ Q 7 6 3
  S     N                    ♠ A K J 8
  2 ◇   2 ♡        N         ♡ 7 5
  5 ◇   —       W     E      ◇ J 10 5 2
                     S       ♣ K J 2
```

West leads the three of spades, your knave wins and South drops the nine. You continue with a second round of spades and South ruffs. Four rounds of trumps are played, your partner showing out on the second round and discarding two spades and a club while three clubs are thrown from dummy. In with the knave of diamonds, how do you continue?

You cannot lead spades and a heart would be dangerous, so the obvious play is the king of clubs to pin dummy's queen. But let's not rush things. Have you counted declarer's tricks? He has six in diamonds, at least three in hearts and the ace of clubs. The danger is that if South has the king of hearts he may make his eleventh trick by finessing against partner's presumed knave. Is there any way of deflecting declarer from this finesse? Yes, a very good way. If you can make him think your partner has the king of clubs he will miscount partner down to three hearts in the end game and play for the drop in hearts. You should therefore lead the knave of clubs.

```
  ♠ 10 6 4 3
  ♡ J 9 3 2        N
  ◇ 7           W     E
  ♣ 9 8 5 4        S

              ♠ 9
              ♡ K 8 4
              ◇ A K Q 8 6 4 3
              ♣ A 10
```

There is virtually no risk in your knave of clubs play, for declarer will not believe that anyone in his right senses would lead knave from king, knave up to a bare queen in dummy.

```
              ♠ K 10
              ♡ J 10 6 2
              ◇ K J 8 4
              ♣ K 7 3
  S      N                      ♠ J 8 4 3
  1 ♡    3 ♡                    ♡ K Q 5
  4 ♡    —                      ◇ 10 2
                               ♣ A J 9 4
```

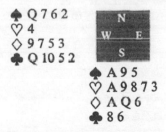

Your partner leads the two of clubs against South's four heart contract, the king is played from dummy and your ace wins. How should you continue?

It looks as though South must have three aces for his bidding. In that case all the defence is likely to make is a heart trick and two clubs, for declarer's normal play will be to run the knave of hearts from dummy. When you have a vulnerable trump holding like this it is always worth while looking for some means of deflecting the declarer from making the orthodox play in the trump suit. In this case your best chance is to switch to the two of diamonds at the second trick. There is no guarantee that it will work, but if declarer believes your two of diamonds to be a singleton he may well abandon the trump finesse and play ace and another.

```
  ♠ Q 7 6 2
  ♡ 4
  ◇ 9 7 5 3
  ♣ Q 10 5 2
              ♠ A 9 5
              ♡ A 9 8 7 3
              ◇ A Q 6
              ♣ 8 6
```

It would be misguided to try to cash the knave of clubs before leading the two of diamonds. Partner might overtake with a masterful air and shoot back a spade or a diamond. No doubt he should not do so, but there is no need for you to put temptation in his way.

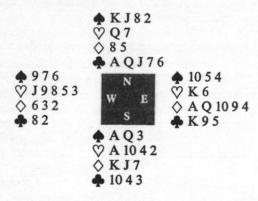

```
♠ 9 7 6        N        N ♣   E ♦   S ♥   W
♡ J 9 8 5 3            1 ♣   1 ♦   1 ♥   —
♦ 6 3 2         W   E   1 ♠   —    3 NT  All pass
♣ 8 2            S
```

From your feeble collection of cards you have to select a lead to defeat South's three no trump contract. Which card do you choose?

The hearts are too weak and your hand too barren of entries to make that a promising lead and there seems little point in leading one of dummy's suits. South's bidding sounds strong but nevertheless your best chance is to lead a diamond, the suit your partner bid. The normal card to play would be the six but, in spite of the fact that your partner has most of the defensive strength, this is a good opportunity to play a false card. If you can persuade declarer that you have a diamond honour he may try to block the suit and knock out your partner's entry immediately. Your best lead is the two of diamonds.

```
                ♠ K J 8 2
                ♡ Q 7
                ♦ 8 5
                ♣ A Q J 7 6
♠ 9 7 6            N          ♠ 10 5 4
♡ J 9 8 5 3                   ♡ K 6
♦ 6 3 2        W     E        ♦ A Q 10 9 4
♣ 8 2             S           ♣ K 9 5
                ♠ A Q 3
                ♡ A 10 4 2
                ♦ K J 7
                ♣ 10 4 3
```

East wins the diamond lead with the ace and returns the ten. If declarer believes you have led from the queen he will go up with the king and play on clubs, intending to knock out East's king before the diamonds can be unblocked. The result will be one down instead of two overtricks.

Hands in which similar bluff tactics can be employed occur quite often. In the 1963 Bermuda Bowl competition the United States pair, Robinson and Jordan, pulled a fast one on the Argentine declarer in this hand.

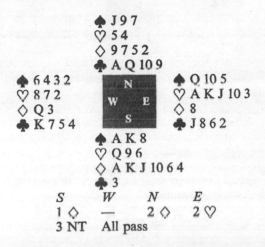

```
                    ♠ J 9 7
                    ♡ 5 4
                    ◇ 9 7 5 2
                    ♣ A Q 10 9
    ♠ 6 4 3 2        ┌───────┐      ♠ Q 10 5
    ♡ 8 7 2          │   N   │      ♡ A K J 10 3
    ◇ Q 3            │ W   E │      ◇ 8
    ♣ K 7 5 4        │   S   │      ♣ J 8 6 2
                    └───────┘
                    ♠ A K 8
                    ♡ Q 9 6
                    ◇ A K J 10 6 4
                    ♣ 3
```

S	W	N	E
1 ◇	—	2 ◇	2 ♡
3 NT	All pass		

Robinson led the two of hearts against the three no trump contract. Jordan won with the ace and returned the knave. Not unreasonably, the declarer took the view that West had led from three to the king and played low in order to block the suit.

Note that neither in this hand nor in the preceding one was there any great risk of misleading partner by the lead of the lowest card from a trebleton. In each case the bidding marked the declarer with a stopper in the suit and it was hardly possible for East to go wrong. When you have a good chance of deceiving declarer without running much risk of inducing misdefence from your partner your false-carding is likely to show a big profit.

Another form of bluff that is very difficult for the declarer to smell out involves the winning of a trick with a higher card than is necessary.

```
                    ♠ J 7 6
                    ♡ 9 3
                    ◊ A K J 10 2
                    ♣ 10 8 5
♠ 8 4 3                            S        N
♡ Q 10 8 5 4        N             1 ♣      1 ◊
◊ Q 6 3         W       E         2 NT     3 NT
♣ A Q              S
```

On your lead of the five of hearts your partner plays the knave and declarer wins with the king. A diamond is led to dummy's ace and the eight of clubs is led and run to you. How do you plan the defence?

It looks as though declarer has the ace of hearts and, on the bidding, his spades must be at least as good as ace and queen. In that case he can certainly make nine tricks by taking a second round diamond finesse. If you win this trick with the queen and knock out the ace of hearts you will leave declarer no alternative but to abandon clubs and try the diamond finesse. Instead you should win with the club ace. This may lead declarer to believe that he has enough tricks without risking the diamond finesse. He will cross to dummy with the diamond king and repeat the club finesse, allowing your bare queen to win. And that will be two down.

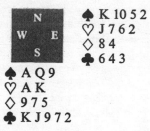

```
                         ♠ K 10 5 2
        N                ♡ J 7 6 2
    W       E            ◊ 8 4
        S                ♣ 6 4 3

        ♠ A Q 9
        ♡ A K
        ◊ 9 7 5
        ♣ K J 9 7 2
```

Although in general it is a complete give-away to hesitate before making a deceptive play, in this case it might not matter if you had to pause to work out the situation. From declarer's point of view you could have been wondering whether to hold up your ace or not.

```
              ♠ Q 9 7 4
              ♡ K 9 3
              ◇ A 8 7 6
              ♣ J 2
  S      N                    ♠ K J 5 2
  1 ♠    3 ♠           N      ♡ J 6 5
  4 ♠    —         W       E  ◇ 10 9 4 2
                         S    ♣ A 3
```

West leads the king of clubs against South's contract of four spades. You overtake and return the three to partner's queen and he continues with the ten of clubs, which is ruffed with dummy's seven. How do you defend?

Most of the declarer's points must be in the red suits, so it looks as though you will have to make two trump tricks to defeat this contract. Is there any point in discarding on this trick in order to preserve a strong trump holding? Not really, for declarer will simply run the queen of spades from dummy and hold his trump losers to one. Partner will never get in again to lead another club. The result will be the same if you win this trick with your trump knave. Declarer will be forced to finesse against the king and will not lose another trick. The only way for you to make two trump tricks is to over-ruff dummy's seven with the king. Provided that it is done smoothly enough declarer will certainly place your partner with the knave. When he gets in he will play the queen of trumps followed by a small one to his ace, and your knave will take the setting trick.

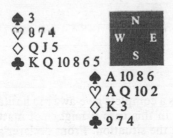

```
  ♠ 3
  ♡ 8 7 4
  ◇ Q J 5                  N
  ♣ K Q 10 8 6 5       W       E
                           S
              ♠ A 10 8 6
              ♡ A Q 10 2
              ◇ K 3
              ♣ 9 7 4
```

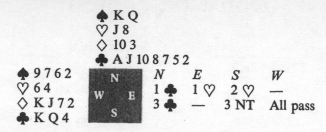

```
              ♠ K Q
              ♡ J 8
              ◇ 10 3
              ♣ A J 10 8 7 5 2
♠ 9 7 6 2                        N     E     S     W
♡ 6 4                           1♣    1♡    2♡    —
◇ K J 7 2                       3♣    —     3 NT  All pass
♣ K Q 4
```

You lead the six of hearts and dummy's knave is covered by your partner's queen which wins the trick. East continues with the ace of hearts, then the two of hearts on which South plays the king. How do you plan the defence?

Prospects are very bleak. On the bidding South is sure to have the aces of spades and diamonds, and with the club honours so favourably placed he looks certain to make his contract. Is there any hope at all for the defence?

There is no certainty of success but, against an imaginative declarer, you should try the effect of discarding your king of clubs on the third round of hearts. It may appear to declarer that you are unblocking from K x in order to create a club entry for your partner. He may therefore abandon clubs and look elsewhere for his tricks.

```
                         ♠ 10 8 5 4
                         ♡ A Q 10 7 5 3
                         ◇ 6 4
                         ♣ 6
              ♠ A J 3
              ♡ K 9 2
              ◇ A Q 9 8 5
              ♣ 9 3
```

If declarer crosses to dummy with a spade and runs the ten of diamonds to your knave, you must follow up your bluff by leading the four of clubs. South is quite likely to put up dummy's ace and lead another diamond, in which case you will make five tricks.

8 · Don't be Fooled!

The defenders have no monopoly on deception, needless to say. Declarers get up to some tricks from time to time and then it is up to you to see that you are not taken in too readily. There is a poker saying, which applies equally well to bridge, to the effect that it is a losing player who is never bluffed. Declarer is bound to get away with some of his duplicity, for there are times when only a defender who is lacking in imagination can fail to be deceived. Nevertheless there are many occasions when attention to detail and a little counting will show you what declarer is up to and point the road to successful defence.

One of the best ways of guarding against trickery is by paying close attention to the small cards that fall. Watching the spots is a valuable habit to acquire, well worth the effort of concentration that is needed. Many an impossible contract has been made because a lazy defender failed to notice the small cards played to the first few tricks. Polish up your spectacles and see if you can defeat this three no trump contract.

```
                    ♠ K J
                    ♡ J 8 3
                    ◇ 8 6 2
                    ♣ A Q 10 9 4
    ♠ 10 6 3                              S        N
    ♡ K 9 5                              1 ♠      2 ♣
    ◇ K Q 10 7 5                         2 NT     3 NT
    ♣ 7 2
```

On your lead of the king of diamonds your partner plays the four and declarer the knave. How do you continue?

Many defenders have gone astray in this situation, on paper at any rate. Were you watching the spots? Then the question that must occur to you is, 'Where is the three of diamonds?' Partner would not play the four from 9 4 3, so the only logical answer is that declarer is concealing the three. If he has played the knave from A J 3 it must be because he wants to make it safe for you to continue diamonds. No doubt he is missing the king of clubs but is sure of nine tricks as long as you do not switch. The only suit he can fear is hearts, therefore you should lead the heart five.

```
                              ♠ 9 7 5 4
                              ♡ Q 10 7 2
                              ◇ 9 4
                              ♣ K 5 3
    ♠ A Q 8 2
    ♡ A 6 4
    ◇ A J 3
    ♣ J 8 6
```

Had declarer's third diamond been a higher card you could not have been sure of what was going on and his deception might well have succeeded. In general it is easier for declarer to conceal a high card than a low one.

```
              ♠ K Q 9 8 3
              ♡ K 7 5
              ◇ J 6
              ♣ 9 7 4
  ♠ J 10 6 5              S      N
  ♡ A 10 2          1 ♡    1 ♠
  ◇ 3 2             3 ◇    3 ♡
  ♣ Q 10 6 3        3 ♠    4 ♠
                    5 ♣    6 ♡
```

You lead the three of clubs against South's slam, your partner producing the king and South the ace. Declarer plays off the ace of spades, your partner following with the four, and then leads the six of hearts. How do you defend?

The play is a little odd. Why did declarer cash the ace of spades? If he has a club loser and intends to throw it on one of dummy's spades you must take your ace of trumps at once and cash the queen of clubs. But there is something that does not add up. If declarer's ace of spades was single partner has played the four from 7 4 2, which is surely not possible. South has the seven of spades, then, and for some reason he is trying to fool you into playing your ace of trumps at once. When you know what declarer wants it is easy enough to do the opposite. You should play the two of hearts to this trick.

```
              ♠ 4 2
              ♡ J 3
              ◇ 10 8 7 5
              ♣ K J 8 5 2
  ♠ A 7
  ♡ Q 9 8 6 4
  ◇ A K Q 9 4
  ♣ A
```

South's bluff might have worked if your partner had not been conscientious about showing his doubleton. Distributional echoes and other defensive signals may help the declarer once in a while but, if you have a counting partner, they will be of far greater value to the defence.

♠ A K Q J 8 6 5
♡ K 9 6 3
◇ —
♣ K 4

♠ 10 9 7 3 2
♡ 8
◇ K Q 9 5
♣ Q J 10

N	S
2 ♠	3 ◇
4 ♣	7 NT

After the above confident, if not very scientific, bidding you lead the king of diamonds against South's grand slam. A spade is thrown from dummy, your partner plays the three and the declarer the ace. South cashes the ace of hearts and continues with the queen and knave. You can spare the five and the nine of diamonds on the second and third round of hearts, but when the declarer leads a fourth heart to dummy's king you are really under pressure in three suits. After some thought you decide to play for partner to have a club stopper and you discard the ten of clubs. Your partner follows to the fourth round of hearts and the declarer eyes your discard with interest. Presently he plays the king of clubs from the table and continues with a small club to his ace. Your worst fears are now realized, for declarer produces the one card you hoped he did not possess—the nine of clubs. What do you discard on this trick?

At this point you have nothing but your five spades and the queen of diamonds left, and dummy has nothing but spades. Your choice of discard is strictly limited and you feel as though you are being put through a mangle. If you are really in the grip of a progressive squeeze there is nothing you can do that will make any difference. But there are still a couple of chances. If you could place your partner with the knave of diamonds, for instance, you could quite happily throw your queen.

Since a slip in defence against a grand slam will be expensive, let us examine carefully the likelihood of your partner having the diamond knave. His distribution would have to be 0-4-4-5 or, less likely, 0-4-5-4 with the eight of clubs. What about the spots? Partner played the three of diamonds to the first trick, did he not? With four or more diamonds headed by the knave he would surely have spared a higher card than the three. With J 4 3 2, for example, he would have played the four. Clearly partner cannot have the knave of diamonds, and it follows that the diamond queen cannot be the proper card for you to throw.

What is left? Can it conceivably defeat the slam if you throw a spade? The only possibility that remains to be considered is that South is void in spades and the spade threat in dummy nothing but a gigantic bluff. Could it be so? It would take some nerve for the declarer to cut himself off from dummy like that. You would have to believe him capable of a great deal of guile. The whole analysis of the position may stretch your credulity to the limit, but if you respect the declarer's dummy play and trust your partner's signals you must discard a spade on the nine of clubs.

```
              ♠ 4
              ♡ 10 7 5 4
              ◇ 7 6 3
              ♣ 8 7 6 5 2
♠ —
♡ A Q J 2
◇ A J 10 8 4 2
♣ A 9 3
```

Declarer's play of the hand was highly competent. It was sound technique to play four rounds of hearts before touching spades, and it soon became abundantly clear from your discards that you were protecting a five-card spade holding. That being so there was no genuine play for the contract and he had to resort to a ruse. It was a fine piece of deception and he was unlucky not to get away with it. He would have succeeded against a defender who did not watch the small cards.

```
              ♠ Q 7 3
              ♡ 9 6
              ◇ J 4 3
              ♣ Q J 10 7 6
Rubber bridge                    ♠ A 8 2
S       N                        ♡ Q 7 4
2 NT    3 NT                     ◇ Q 10 9 7 5
                                 ♣ 9 3
```

You are partnered by a stranger, of whose methods you know very little. He leads the three of hearts against South's three no trump contract and your queen is taken by South's king. The declarer cashes the ace and king of clubs, your partner playing the two and five, and then leads the king of spades. What do you do?

Is declarer trying to create an entry to dummy? If so you can certainly keep him out by holding up your ace. What about the club position? If your partner had four clubs he might have echoed, but you cannot be certain that this particular partner would. In point of fact it does not matter if your partner has never heard of an echo, for there is a simpler guide to the situation. The four of clubs is missing and, unless your partner is playing very unnaturally, the declarer must have it. He must be trying to steal his ninth trick with the king of spades, so you should win at once and return the seven of hearts.

```
♠ J 9 6              
♡ A 10 5 3 2         
◇ 8 2                
♣ 8 5 2              
              ♠ K 10 5 4
              ♡ K J 8
              ◇ A K 6
              ♣ A K 4
```

When there is no useful information to be obtained from the small cards, often the line of play adopted by declarer will itself point the way to a successful defence. Any unusual play by declarer should be carefully studied, for inferences abound in such situations.

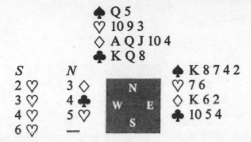

♠ Q 5
♡ 10 9 3
◇ A Q J 10 4
♣ K Q 8

S	N		♠ K 8 7 4 2
2 ♡	3 ◇		♡ 7 6
3 ♡	4 ♣		◇ K 6 2
4 ♡	5 ♡		♣ 10 5 4
6 ♡	—		

Your partner's lead of the knave of spades is covered by the queen, king and ace. The declarer leads a diamond and finesses dummy's ten to your king. How do you continue?

There are only two possibilities. You must either lead a club, playing partner for the ace, or you must cash a spade trick. The declarer's failure to draw trumps might be taken as an indication that he is missing the ace of clubs and scared of a signal from your partner, but the play of the spade queen from dummy suggests that he has a spade loser. Let us analyse further. If declarer has the ace of clubs it must be accompanied by two small cards, otherwise he could get a discard on dummy's clubs. He must have a doubleton diamond for the finesse to make sense. If he has only six hearts that just leaves room for a doubleton spade in his hand. But with that hand a declarer acute enough to finesse diamonds before drawing trumps would surely not have played the queen of spades from dummy on the first trick. The obvious play would be to duck in dummy and win with the ace, draw trumps, eliminate clubs and exit with the spade, forcing you to lead a diamond or give him a ruff and discard. Then declarer's ace of spades was single and the play of the queen from dummy just a piece of camouflage. You must therefore lead a club to your partner's ace.

♠ J 10 9 6 3
♡ 4
◇ 9 8 5
♣ A 9 7 6

♠ A
♡ A K Q J 8 5 2
◇ 7 3
♣ J 3 2

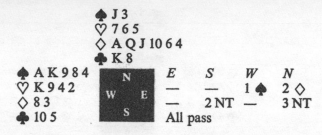

```
            ♠ J 3
            ♡ 7 6 5
            ◇ A Q J 10 6 4
            ♣ K 8
♠ A K 9 8 4                      E    S    W    N
♡ K 9 4 2                        —    —    1♠   2◇
◇ 8 3                            —    2 NT  —   3 NT
♣ 10 5                           All pass
```

You make a dubious opening lead of the ace of spades against South's three no trump contract. After examining dummy you switch to the two of hearts, on which partner plays the ten and declarer the ace. South plays a further spade which you win with the king, East following. How do you continue?

It looks as though you can defeat this contract by taking three heart tricks, but declarers have been known to win with the ace when holding the queen as well so you had better examine all possibilities. You can be quite sure that declarer does not have both the king of diamonds and the ace of clubs. That would give him a thirteen point hand, which few players pass nowadays. More conclusive is that with the two key cards he would have nine top tricks and would not be messing about with spades. A diamond lead will be fatal if declarer has the king, for six diamonds, two spades and a heart will be all the tricks he needs. What about a club lead? That will be fatal only if declarer has a five-card club suit headed by A Q J, or a six-card suit headed by A J. But with either of these holdings South would certainly have opened the bidding. The club ten is therefore your proper lead.

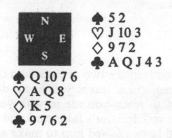

```
                ♠ 5 2
                ♡ J 10 3
                ◇ 9 7 2
                ♣ A Q J 4 3
          ♠ Q 10 7 6
          ♡ A Q 8
          ◇ K 5
          ♣ 9 7 6 2
```

The club lead will win eight tricks for the defence and make South sorry he tried that particular bluff.

♠ 10 9 7 2
♡ A 2
◇ K Q 9 4
♣ A J 3

♠ K Q 6
♡ Q J 10 5
◇ 10 3
♣ Q 10 5 2

Match-point pairs

S	N
1 NT[1]	2 ♣
2 ♠	4 ♠
—	

You lead the queen of hearts against South's four spade contract. The ace is played from dummy, your partner following with the six and declarer with the seven. Dummy's ten of spades is now run to your queen. How do you continue?

In view of the strong dummy you are unlikely to beat this contract. It looks as though you will take exactly three tricks—two trumps and a heart. However, it might be unwise to assume too readily that you can cash a heart. Since you still have trump control there can be no harm in leading a club at this stage. The club lead could only be wrong if South had a doubleton heart along with doubleton king of clubs, which is hardly possible on the bidding. Besides, if South had only two hearts your partner could have spared a higher heart to echo with.

♠ 5 4
♡ 9 8 6
◇ 8 7 5 2
♣ K 9 7 4

♠ A J 8 3
♡ K 7 4 3
◇ A J 6
♣ 8 6

When you lead the two of clubs and dummy wins with the ace, your partner's nine leaves you in no doubt as to which suit to continue with when you are in with your second trump. If you had swallowed declarer's false card and led a heart at trick three that would have allowed him to make an easy overtrick.

[1] 12–14 points.

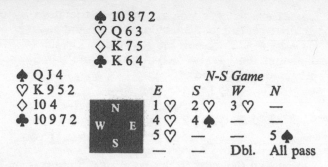

♠ 10 8 7 2
♡ Q 6 3
◇ K 7 5
♣ K 6 4

♠ Q J 4   *N-S Game*
♡ K 9 5 2 | E | S | W | N |
◇ 10 4 |---|---|---|---|
♣ 10 9 7 2 | 1 ♡ | 2 ♡ | 3 ♡ | — |
                   | 4 ♡ | 4 ♠ | — | — |
                   | 5 ♡ | — | — | 5 ♠ |
                   | — | — | Dbl. | All pass |

After the above contentious auction you lead the two of hearts against South's doubled contract of five spades. Your partner plays the ten and South ruffs with the three of spades. Declarer now makes you blink by leading the five of spades from his hand. It requires no deep analysis to play your knave, and your partner follows suit with the six. How should you continue?

Declarer's line of play is surely a little odd. What can he be up to? He cannot have been hoping to slip past the queen and knave of trumps, so why has he played trumps in such an unorthodox manner? The only logical explanation is that he expected to lose a trump trick anyway and has craftily chose to do so at a time when your partner is unable to indicate where his outside strength lies. No doubt you will be able to take two tricks in one of the minor suits if you lead the right one immediately. But how can you tell which to lead?

This is another occasion when your defence has to be based on a hypothetical count. You know from the bidding that the declarer's hand will be unbalanced, but if discards on his long suit are going to do him any good he must be extremely unbalanced. For a wrong guess by you to give him his contract declarer will have to be 5-0-6-2 or 5-0-2-6 in shape, and you must therefore defend on the assumption that it is so. A study of your minor suit-lengths will tell you which of these distributions is possible. If your partner had six diamonds to the ace and queen and a void in clubs he would not have stopped bidding at the five level. Then diamonds must be the declarer's suit and it follows that your proper lead at this point is a club.

♠ 6
♡ A J 10 8 7 4
♢ 8 2
♣ A Q 5 3

♠ A K 9 5 3
♡ —
♢ A Q J 9 6 3
♣ J 8

Having placed you with a trump trick on the bidding, declarer played well in giving you it immediately without affording your partner a chance to signal. If you had returned anything but a club after making your knave of spades declarer would have drawn the outstanding trumps, discarded all dummy's clubs on the diamonds and ruffed a club in dummy, thus making eleven tricks.

A point which has been mentioned before will bear repeating. You could have saved yourself some brain fatigue on this hand by making a better tactical opening lead. In defence against a suit contract when you have four or more cards headed by an honour in a suit in which you know your partner has length, it is often best to lead the honour card. This applies particularly when you wish to hold the lead and have a look at dummy before deciding on your switch. In this case the lead of the king of hearts would not allow you to hold the lead, but it would give your partner the opportunity of making a suit preference signal by following with the four. Then on regaining the lead with the knave of spades you would have no difficulty in finding the killing return.

♠ A J 7
♡ K 8 3
◇ Q 9 3
♣ J 10 6 2

♠ 6 5
♡ J 10 2
◇ 8 7 4
♣ K Q 9 8 7

	S	N
	1 ♠	2 NT
	6 ♠	

Against South's boldly bid spade slam you lead the king of clubs. Your partner follows with the three and the declarer wins with the ace. A spade is led to dummy's ace and your partner plays the ten. Now comes the knave of clubs from dummy, on which your partner plays the four and declarer discards the five of hearts. On winning with the queen what do you lead?

Once again the fact that declarer has not drawn all the trumps might be taken as an indication that he fears a signal from your partner. If declarer has seven spades that leaves him with only five cards in the red suits. Can he be planning to throw another heart on the ten of clubs? A moment's reflection will tell you that this is highly unlikely. With a small doubleton in hearts declarer would be mad to mess about like this. His proper play would be to bank on the ace of hearts being in your hand. Then declarer must be trying to induce a heart lead from you, and on that reasoning you must lead a diamond. If your partner is a reliable suit preference signaller you have a further indication in the fact that he played the lower of his remaining clubs on the knave.

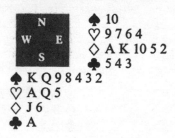

♠ 10
♡ 9 7 6 4
◇ A K 10 5 2
♣ 5 4 3

♠ K Q 9 8 4 3 2
♡ A Q 5
◇ J 6
♣ A

♠ K 9 3
♡ Q 2
◇ Q 10 9 7 5 4
♣ 8 4

		W	N	E	S
♠ A J 8		1 NT	—	—	3 ♡
♡ 9 6 5		—	4 ♡	All pass	
◇ A K 3					
♣ Q 10 6 2					

You lead the ace of diamonds against South's four heart contract. Your partner plays the two and declarer the eight, and you hastily switch to a trump. Declarer captures your partner's eight with the ten and leads the seven of spades. How do you plan the defence?

What is declarer up to? This spade lead before drawing trumps seems a little odd. Could it be a singleton? No, of course not, for your partner would certainly have taken out your one no trump bid with six spades to the queen. Then there can be no hurry to make your ace, but there must be some reason for this spade play. The most likely explanation is that declarer has the queen and ten of spades and is trying to utilize dummy's nine as an extra entry so that he can ruff out the diamonds. In that case the one card you must not play to this trick is the eight. Either the knave or the ace will serve to block the spade suit, but the knave is the proper card to play since it also caters for the possibility that declarer does not have the ten of spades. With Q x x he could be trying to hustle you into playing the ace.

♠ 6 5 4 2
♡ 8 3
◇ J 6 2
♣ K J 7 3

♠ Q 10 7
♡ A K J 10 7 4
◇ 8
♣ A 9 5

If South had won the first trump in dummy, ruffed a diamond immediately and drawn trumps before leading the spade, the blocking play would have been easier for you to spot.

♠ 6 2
♡ 9 4 3
◇ K 8 7 5 4 2
♣ J 5

♠ Q J 10 8 5   *S*   *N*
♡ Q 10 7 6   2 ♣   2 ◇
◇ J 3   2 NT   3 NT
♣ 9 8   —

You lead the queen of spades against South's three no trump contract, your partner playing the nine and the declarer the four. You continue with the knave of spades, partner covers with the king and South's ace takes the trick. Surprisingly, the declarer now leads the seven of spades. What do you make of that?

Such generosity must always be suspect. The declarer will not be making you a present of your remaining spade tricks without some fiendish purpose in mind. Perhaps he is preparing the ground for a minor suit squeeze on your partner, or it may be that there is a blockage in the diamond position. There is no need to look too deeply into the problem at this stage. It is enough to know that the declarer wants you to continue with spades. What is good for the declarer must be bad for the defence, therefore you should switch after winning the third round of spades. Why not cash a fourth spade while retaining the fifth to avoid rectifying the count for a possible squeeze? That might work out all right if you could be certain it was a squeeze that declarer was planning, but cashing a fourth spade would be fatal if it allowed declarer to unblock the diamond suit.

Let us assume that you decide to switch at trick four and lead the nine of clubs which is covered by the knave, queen and ace. Looking peeved, declarer leads the nine of diamonds. What do you do now?

That play of the nine of diamonds is a sure indication that declarer's diamond holding is A 10 9. Then it was a diamond discard he was angling for when he continued spades. Now he will be hoping to be allowed to duck this diamond trick to your partner who has no more spades. You must dash his hopes by playing your knave. This will hold declarer to three tricks in the diamond suit and he will be unable to make his contract.

♠ K 9 3
♡ 8 2
◇ Q 6
♣ Q 10 7 6 3 2

♠ A 7 4
♡ A K J 5
◇ A 10 9
♣ A K 4

Instead of putting you to the test by leading the nine of diamonds the declarer might have probed your partner's defence by leading the ace. It should not be too difficult for East to work out that it would be dangerous to hang on to his queen.

9 • Counting Again

In a bridge book where the primary classification is not done on a technical basis the chapters tend to overlap. There are a great many hands that might be classified under any one of several headings, and the chapters on counting provide a useful clearing-house for these. Some of the hands that follow may require close partnership co-operation, some contain an element of deception, in some the defence must rely on inferences drawn from the declarer's line of play. But, as always, counting of one kind or another has a part to play in finding the correct defence.

♠ A J 9 4
♡ Q 7 6
◇ K 5 2
♣ J 4 3

S	N		♠ 6 5 2
1 ◇	1 ♠		♡ K 8 3
1 NT[1]	3 NT		◇ 7 4
			♣ A Q 9 7 5

West leads the two of hearts against South's three no trump contract, the six is played from dummy and declarer plays the five on your king. How should you continue?

Prospects for the defence are not very hopeful. If your partner has the ace of hearts he cannot hold more than a knave outside. It is just conceivable that he has a diamond stopper. If you return a heart your partner, having no outside entry, will duck. One heart, four spades and three diamonds will give the declarer eight tricks and the king of clubs will be his ninth. Since you cannot defeat the contract by continuing hearts you must try the club suit. Partner will have to have the ten of clubs. You must lead the queen, and if declarer wins with the king your partner must unblock by throwing his ten.

♠ 10 8 7
♡ A 9 4 2
◇ J 10 8 3
♣ 10 2

♠ K Q 3
♡ J 10 5
◇ A Q 9 6
♣ K 8 6

If declarer allows your queen of clubs to hold the trick you can switch back to hearts, and the defence will gather in five tricks before declarer can make nine.

[1] 15–16 points.

♠ K J 10 6
♡ K 3
◇ 8 4 3
♣ A K 7 2

```
S       N
1 NT¹   2 ♣
2 ◇     3 NT
```

♠ 9 8 5 2
♡ Q 8 4
◇ K J 7
♣ Q J 3

Your partner leads the knave of hearts against South's three no trump contract. The three is played from dummy, you encourage with the eight and South plays the two. West continues with the nine of hearts, and you drop your queen under dummy's king. The three of diamonds is now led from dummy. How do you plan the defence?

Dummy is quite strong and the outlook for the defence far from hopeful. But if South's opening bid was a minimum there is just room for your partner to hold an ace. Indeed he will have to hold an ace if the contract is to be defeated, and it is not hard to see that the ace of spades will not be good enough. After finessing the queen of diamonds declarer will switch, and three tricks in spades along with two in each other suit will see him home. Then partner must have the ace of diamonds, in which case the killing defence is obvious. You must go up with your king of diamonds and knock out the ace of hearts while your partner still has an entry.

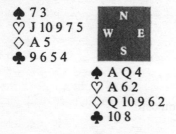

♠ 7 3
♡ J 10 9 7 5
◇ A 5
♣ 9 6 5 4

♠ A Q 4
♡ A 6 2
◇ Q 10 9 6 2
♣ 10 8

You might in any case have read your partner's nine of hearts at trick two as a suit preference signal indicating an entry into diamonds.

¹ 12–14 points.

♠ Q 9 5
♡ A Q 9 2
◇ A 6
♣ A Q 9 4

♠ 2
♡ J 6 4
◇ Q J 9 5 2
♣ 8 5 3 2

N	E	S	W
1 ♣	1 ♠	1 NT	—
3 NT	All pass		

You lead the two of spades against South's three no trump contract. Your partner wins with the ace and returns the knave, on which South plays the king and you discard a club. A heart is led for a finesse and dummy's queen is captured by your partner's king. East continues with the eight of spades and the declarer follows with the ten. How do you plan the defence?

With both of the minor suit kings South is sure to make his contract, but he may have only one. If it is the king of diamonds you have probably nothing to worry about, but if it is the king of clubs the situation is not so good. Declarer will have eight top tricks and will need to develop only one trick in hearts to get home. If he has the ten of hearts you will not be able to prevent him establishing the heart trick he needs, but your partner could have that card. You must therefore ditch that dangerous knave of hearts on the third round of spades and thus prevent declarer from ducking a heart into your hand.

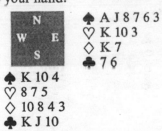

♠ A J 8 7 6 3
♡ K 10 3
◇ K 7
♣ 7 6

♠ K 10 4
♡ 8 7 5
◇ 10 8 4 3
♣ K J 10

Unless the knave of hearts is discarded the declarer will make his contract by playing the hearts so as to keep East out of the lead.

♠ K
♡ A J 10 9 3
◇ A 10 8 7 5
♣ J 4

S	N
1 ♠	2 ♡
2 ♠	3 ◇
3 NT	—

♠ Q 10 5 4
♡ Q 8 6 2
◇ 9 3
♣ Q 7 6

Your partner's lead of the king of diamonds is ducked. West switches to the ten of clubs, and dummy's knave is covered by your queen and declarer's king. South leads the four of hearts on which West plays the five and dummy the nine. How do you plan the defence?

On the bidding South must surely have the two black aces, but your partner is pretty well marked with the king of hearts. If South had held that card he would have played off the king of spades before tackling the hearts in order to avoid any entry trouble. Declarer would not attack hearts if he held a singleton, so you can be sure your partner's king is going to fall under the ace on the next round. South therefore has two spades, four hearts, a diamond and two clubs, making nine tricks in all, but because of the spade blockage he may not be able to take them. You must cut the last line of communication between the table and declarer's hand by winning your heart trick immediately and leading the seven of clubs.

♠ 7 6 2
♡ K 5
◇ K Q J 6
♣ 10 9 8 3

♠ A J 9 8 3
♡ 7 4
◇ 4 2
♣ A K 5 2

Note that it would be fatal to duck a round of hearts. That would permit the declarer to unblock in spades before forcing out your queen of hearts.

```
              ♠ K Q 5
              ♡ Q 8 3
              ◇ J 7
              ♣ 9 7 6 4 3
♠ 10 7 6 2                        S        N
♡ K 4                            1 ♡      2 ♡
◇ K 10 9 6 4                     3 ◇      3 NT
♣ J 5                            4 ♡       —
```

You lead the knave of clubs against South's four heart contract, your partner plays the eight and South wins with the ace. The declarer plays off the ace of spades and continues with the knave to dummy's queen. On the third round of spades he discards the two of clubs from his hand. Dummy's knave of diamonds is now run to your king. How should you continue?

Declarer's distribution appears to be 2-5-4-2. He must have the ace and queen of diamonds, for partner would not have played low with a doubleton honour. It looks as though South intends to ruff a diamond in dummy, but he may get an unpleasant shock to find your partner over-ruffing. If you exit with your remaining club at this point you may be able to get a defensive cross-ruff going. In order to over-ruff dummy twice your partner's trumps would have to be as good as A 9 x, which is not impossible. But what are you thinking of? If partner has the ace of trumps there is no need for him to have the nine as well. You can defeat the contract quite simply by drawing trumps so that declarer is left with a losing diamond. Your proper lead is therefore the king of hearts.

```
                          ♠ 9 8 4 3
                          ♡ A 7 2
                          ◇ 5 2
                          ♣ K Q 10 8
              ♠ A J
              ♡ J 10 9 6 5
              ◇ A Q 8 3
              ♣ A 2
```

```
                    ♠ 9 5
                    ♡ J 9 7 6 3
                    ◇ K J
                    ♣ Q 8 7 4
        N-S game                      ♠ 7 2
  S     W     N     E                 ♡ Q 8 4
  1◇    1♠    —     2♣                ◇ 10 3
  2♡    2♠    4♡    All pass          ♣ A J 9 6 5 2
```

Your partner leads the king of clubs against South's four heart contract. How do you plan the defence?

The first question to ask yourself is whether your partner's king of clubs is a singleton or not. You know that the declarer will have more diamonds than hearts, which accounts for at least nine of his cards. If he has a doubleton club that leaves room for only two spades. But with seven spades, at this vulnerability, your partner might well have made a pre-emptive bid of three spades over the diamond opening.

In any case if declarer has two clubs the position looks pretty hopeless, for you will never get in to cash your second club trick. Even if you overtake and give partner a ruff it is unlikely that the defence will be able to scrape up another two tricks. The best chance is that declarer has a singleton club and three spades to the king. You should overtake your partner's club king with the ace and return a spade, hoping to make one club, two spades and a spade ruff with your queen of hearts.

```
        ♠ A Q 10 8 4 3
        ♡ 2
        ◇ 9 7 6 5
        ♣ K 3

              ♠ K J 6
              ♡ A K 10 5
              ◇ A Q 8 4 2
              ♣ 10
```

♠ Q 10 8
♡ 7 4
◇ A K 9 6 2
♣ K J 10

♠ A J 7 2
♡ K 10 5 3
◇ 8 5 3
♣ A 8

Game all

N	S
1 ◇	1 NT

You lead the three of hearts against South's contract of one no trump, your partner playing the queen and South the ace. A club is led to dummy's king and a club returned to your ace, East following with the two and three. How should you continue?

It looks as though South started with five clubs headed by the queen, in which case he can take seven tricks as soon as he gets in. Is there any chance of the defence making seven tricks first? Since declarer has the queen of clubs and ace and knave of hearts, he is unlikely to have the spade king. If your partner has the nine of spades as well as the king it will be possible to give declarer a difficult guess. You should lead the knave of spades, which will be covered by the queen and king. On regaining the lead with a heart you will continue with a small spade, and if South guesses wrong he will make only five tricks.

♠ K 9 3
♡ Q 8 6 2
◇ Q 10 7
♣ 6 3 2

♠ 6 5 4
♡ A J 9
◇ J 4
♣ Q 9 7 5 4

At match-point pairs, of course, it would be needlessly risky to defend like that. Since you can work out that a two heart contract by East-West would go one down, you would be happy enough to allow South to score ninety points.

```
                    ♠ K J 6
                    ♡ 5
                    ♦ J 10 9 7 5 3 2
                    ♣ 6 2
    Game all                            ♠ Q 10 9 8 7 5 3 2
 E    S    W    N                       ♡ K 7
 3 ♠  3 NT  All pass                    ♦ K 4
                                        ♣ J
```

West leads the queen of hearts and your king is allowed to hold the trick. You return the seven, declarer plays low and your partner wins with the knave and continues with the nine. How do you plan the defence?

Clearly there is no hope unless your partner's hearts can be brought in and you must therefore make sure that entry to your partner's hand is not blocked. West may well have the queen of diamonds, in fact he will have to have queen and another diamond if the contract is to be defeated, but there is no desperate hurry to get rid of your diamond king. Since dummy has only one entry your king of diamonds can always be thrown under the ace.

The dangerous card in your hand is the knave of clubs. South is marked with length and strength in clubs, and although your partner may have a stopper his holding could be as weak as 10 x x x. You must jettison your knave of clubs on the third round of hearts before it can endanger the defence.

```
 ♠ —
 ♡ Q J 10 9 6 3 2
 ♦ Q 6
 ♣ 10 9 7 3
                    ♠ A 4
                    ♡ A 8 4
                    ♦ A 8
                    ♣ A K Q 8 5 4
```

Better bidding might have led to the superior contract of five diamonds. In three no trumps if South had been inspired enough to win the second round of hearts, cross to the king of spades and lead a club, he could have made his contract by allowing your knave to hold the trick.

```
              ♠ A 5
              ♡ J 6
              ◇ 10 3 2
              ♣ K Q J 8 6 3
♠ Q 9 8 2                      W    N    E    S
♡ A 3                          1◇   2♣   —    2 NT
◇ A K J 8                      —    3 NT  All pass
♣ A 10 9
```

Although puce in the face, you refrain from doubling and lead the two of spades against South's three no trump contract. The five is played from dummy, your partner plays the ten and South the knave. A club is led and dummy's knave wins. The king of clubs is now led and your partner discards the two of hearts. How do you plan your defence?

Declarer must have all the outstanding face cards, which makes this in effect a double dummy problem. Since dummy has an entry in the ace of spades it might seem that it can make no difference whether you hold up your ace of clubs until the third round or not. In fact the difference is crucial. If you take your ace on the second round and lead a spade you allow declarer to preserve a line of communication. He will next play a heart to his queen and you will be unable to stop him from making nine tricks. If, on the other hand, you keep your ace of clubs until the third round before knocking out dummy's spade ace, declarer will be in an unhappy dilemma. He will have the choice of abandoning two winning clubs on the table or inflicting a suicide squeeze on himself by running all the clubs. Whatever he tries you will be able to hold him to eight tricks.

```
                        ♠ 10 7 4 3
                        ♡ 10 9 8 7 5 2
                        ◇ 7 4
                        ♣ 5
              ♠ K J 6
              ♡ K Q 4
              ◇ Q 9 6 5
              ♣ 7 4 2
```

```
                    ♠ K 7
                    ♡ A K 10 7
                    ◇ 8 5
                    ♣ A K Q 10 2
      Game all                      ♠ 2
     N      S           N           ♡ Q 9 5 4 2
     1♣     1♠      W       E        ◇ Q 4 3
     2♡     2♠          S            ♣ 8 7 6 5
     4♠     —
```

West leads the ace of diamonds against South's contract of four spades, you encourage in so far as you can with the four and declarer plays the two. West switches to the three of clubs, won by dummy's ace. Declarer plays off the king and ace of spades and looks disgruntled when you discard a heart. He leads the six of hearts to the ace, your partner playing the three, and continues with the king of hearts, on which he throws the six of diamonds while your partner follows with the eight. Now the seven of hearts is led from dummy. How do you plan your defence?

What do you think declarer is up to? Why is he messing about with hearts instead of drawing the outstanding trumps? There can be only one answer. Your partner must have queen and another trump left and declarer is trying to avoid a club ruff. He intends to discard his remaining diamond on this heart, thus cutting the defensive communications and preventing your partner from putting you in with a diamond to give him the club ruff. Although your partner has slipped up in failing to unblock in hearts, you can recover by playing your queen on this trick. This will make dummy's ten of hearts high, but it will do the declarer no good for he will be unable to avoid the club ruff.

```
     ♠ Q 6 4 3            N
     ♡ J 8 3          W       E
     ◇ A K J 10 7         S
     ♣ 3
                    ♠ A J 10 9 8 5
                    ♡ 6
                    ◇ 9 6 2
                    ♣ J 9 4
```

Defensive problems of this kind are easy enough to solve on paper, and I expect most readers got that one right. But when the hand was played in the quarter-finals of the 1965 Gold Cup competition the defenders failed to come up with the right answer.

10 • End-Game Defence

Some hands involving end-game defence have appeared, for one reason or another, in earlier chapters. Now we are going to examine the subject in closer detail. In this chapter we shall concentrate exclusively on the defence to throw-in and elimination play and the defence to trump coups. Squeeze defence is examined in a separate chapter.

No special technique is required. As always it is by careful counting and logical deduction that the defenders keep themselves aware of what is going on. In this phase of defence perhaps the most useful quality to cultivate is that of foresight, for early recognition is half the battle. It is necessary to look ahead and see the end-play coming in order to be able to take effective counter-measures. Although the term might seem to imply the play to the last few tricks, an end-play can materialize quite early in the play of the hand. Indeed it is possible for a defender to be end-played on the opening lead. Fortunately that does not happen very often. Usually there will be a little room for manœuvre, but very often the chance of a successful line of defence has to be seized during the play to the first few tricks of the hand. Many defenders see the danger too late, when the end-play is already upon them.

The chief defence to throw-in play lies in unblocking. Everybody likes to hold high cards and for a beginner it would be unthinkable to throw them away. But as a player's bridge education progresses he comes to realize that there are times when high cards are a liability rather than an asset, times when he must get rid of his high cards without delay in order to avoid being thrown in to make a fatal lead.

The danger signs are not hard to read and a defender soon learns what to look out for. When most of the defensive strength is concentrated in one hand the holder of that hand must tread warily. He will be on lead several times and may have to plan his play with care to avoid being thrown in. As soon as it is clear to a defender that he has a vulnerable tenace holding in a certain suit a warning buzzer should sound. He must make up his mind that, come what may, he will not allow himself to be thrown in to lead from that holding.

There will be occasions, of course, where no successful defence is possible. The cards will be so arranged that the declarer will make his contract no matter what you do, and you will have to smile and pretend to like it. But, if you keep awake and cultivate the habit of looking ahead, you will find that in a surprisingly large number of hands an effective defence is present, just waiting to be spotted.

```
                    ♠ A 7 4 3
                    ♡ 10 6 5 3
                    ◇ Q 8
                    ♣ A K J
    S      N                        ♠ K 5
    1 ♡    4 ♣                      ♡ K 7
    4 ♡    —                        ◇ K J 6 4 3
                                    ♣ 9 8 6 2
```

North's bid of four clubs is one version of the Swiss Convention, showing a strong raise to four hearts.

West leads the queen of spades against the four heart contract. Dummy plays low and you overtake with the king and return the five, your partner's eight forcing dummy's ace. The three of hearts is now led from the table. How do you defend?

Do you recognize the danger signs? The declarer must have both red aces for his bid, and if you play low to this trick he will win with the ace, eliminate clubs and put you in with the king of hearts to make a minor suit lead that will give him an extra trick. To avoid this fate you must play your king of hearts immediately.

```
    ♠ Q J 9 8
    ♡ Q 2
    ◇ 10 9 7 2
    ♣ 10 5 4
                        ♠ 10 6 2
                        ♡ A J 9 8 4
                        ◇ A 5
                        ♣ Q 7 3
```

Perhaps you think that one too easy. Unblocking plays do tend to look obvious when presented on paper, but I wonder if you would have found it at the table. The play of the king looks as though it could be dangerous if your partner has a singleton queen, but that is an illusion. If declarer has six trumps to the ace he is going to make eleven tricks whatever you do. The play of the king of hearts merely trades a trump trick for a diamond or a spade.

```
              ♠ A K
              ♡ A K 9 7 5 2
              ◇ K 7 6 4
              ♣ 7
♠ J 3                            N      S
♡ 4                             1 ♡    1 ♠
◇ J 9 5 3                       3 ♡    3 NT
♣ Q 10 8 5 4 2                  —
```

You lead the five of clubs and East wins with the ace, declarer playing the three. The six of clubs return is covered by declarer's knave and won by your queen, dummy shedding a heart. How do you continue?

That heart discard from dummy could be an indication that declarer will be relying on spade tricks for his contract. If so you may be able to disrupt his communications by attacking diamonds before the spades are unblocked. However, if you are looking ahead you will lead not the normal three of diamonds but the five. This is not, of course, a deceptive play. It is an early unblocking move to guard against a throw-in.

```
                          ♠ Q 10 6
                          ♡ Q J 10 8 3
                          ◇ 10 8 2
                          ♣ A 6
              ♠ 9 8 7 5 4 2
              ♡ 6
              ◇ A Q
              ♣ K J 9 3
```

On winning the diamond lead declarer will play two rounds of hearts. When that suit fails to break he will try to throw you in with the fourth round of diamonds to lead from your minor tenace in clubs. Having taken precautions you are now in no difficulty. If declarer fails to cash his king of clubs you continue to unblock in diamonds. South will make two spade, two heart and four diamond tricks, but your partner must get three hearts at the end. Note that if you lead the diamond three at trick three all declarer need do to ensure success is to preserve dummy's four of diamonds as an exit card.

South could have made his contract by winning the second

club and playing on spades, but the clubs might well have been 5-3. The superior contract of four spades is not easy to reach.

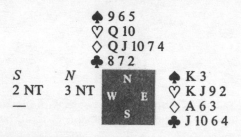

```
              ♠ 9 6 5
              ♡ Q 10
              ◊ Q J 10 7 4
              ♣ 8 7 2
 S      N                    ♠ K 3
 2 NT   3 NT                 ♡ K J 9 2
 —                           ◊ A 6 3
                             ♣ J 10 6 4
```

Your partner leads the queen of spades against South's three no trump contract, and your king is allowed to hold the trick. How should you continue?

A casual glance tells you that there is nothing to worry about here. The declarer is certainly going down in his contract. You can hold up your ace of diamonds for as long as is necessary, and since your heart honours are favourably placed declarer will have no means of access to dummy's long diamonds. Or will he?

Closer examination shows that the situation is fraught with danger. The declarer's twenty points must be composed of the two major aces, the king of diamonds and the three top clubs. In that case the unthinking return of the three of spades will lead to a certain throw-in. The declarer will win with the ace, cash his top clubs and play on diamonds. When you take your ace you will be able to cash the knave of clubs but will then have to lead a red suit and present declarer with his contract .To break up the end-play position you must lead the two of hearts immediately. You can afford to allow dummy to make a heart trick at this stage, but not after the diamonds have been established.

```
 ♠ Q J 10 7 2
 ♡ 7 6 5
 ◊ 8 5 2
 ♣ 9 5

              ♠ A 8 4
              ♡ A 8 4 3
              ◊ K 9
              ♣ A K Q 3
```

♠ K 9 7 4
♡ 8 6
◇ 9 8 6 3
♣ J 9 2

♠ A 5
♡ K 10 4 2
◇ A K 7 5
♣ Q 8 3

S	W	N	E
1 ♠	Dbl.	2 ♠	—
4 ♠	All pass		

You lead the ace of diamonds against South's four spade contract, your partner playing the queen and declarer the two. How should you continue?

Your partner's queen of diamonds tells you that it is safe to underlead your king on the second round. It would be very profitable if you could put him in with his knave of diamonds to lead a heart through. But that is fairy-tale stuff. In real life things do not work out so easily. On the bidding it is most unlikely that declarer has a second diamond, and a little reflection will convince you that it would be anything but safe to lead a second round of diamonds at this point. Declarer might then have enough trump entries in dummy to eliminate your diamonds before throwing you in to make a fatal lead. You must switch at trick two in order to preserve an exit card for the later stages. A heart or a club lead would also be highly dangerous, so your proper lead is the ace and another trump.

♠ 6
♡ J 9 7 3
◇ Q J 10 4
♣ 10 6 5 4

♠ Q J 10 8 3 2
♡ A Q 5
◇ 2
♣ A K 7

A diamond continuation at trick two would allow declarer to get home by a combination of reverse dummy and throw-in play. After ruffing out your diamonds he would put you in with the third round of clubs to lead up to his major tenace in hearts.

```
                         ♠ A K 7 6
                         ♡ K 8 6 5 3
                         ♢ 9 6
                         ♣ A K
     N-S game                             ♠ 3
  W    N    E    S          N             ♡ Q 10 9 4
  4♢   Dbl. 5♢   5♠       W     E         ♢ 10 7
  All pass                   S            ♣ Q J 9 6 3 2
```

West leads the seven of clubs against South's contract of five
spades. Declarer draws two rounds of trumps with the ace and
queen and your partner follows. A club is led to the ace, your
partner playing the eight, and the three of hearts is led from
dummy. How do you defend?

Have you been counting? Then you will know that since West
has shown up with three clubs and a doubleton spade in addition
to at least seven diamonds he cannot have more than a singleton
heart. If his heart is a small card the position is hopeless. Declarer
will finesse the knave, ruff out the hearts and make an overtrick.
If partner's heart is the ace his diamonds will not be better than
K J 10 and again declarer will make his contract. The only cards
partner may have that offer any hope for the defence are the
knave of hearts and ace and queen of diamonds. You must therefore play your queen on this trick to prevent declarer from ducking.

```
  ♠ 9 2
  ♡ J                        N
  ♢ A Q J 8 5 4 3        W       E
  ♣ 8 7 4                   S
                  ♠ Q J 10 8 5 4
                  ♡ A 7 2
                  ♢ K 2
                  ♣ 10 5
```

The declarer will not like your queen of hearts play, but he will
probably win with the ace and exit with the king of diamonds.
On winning, your partner will have to show a little faith by underleading his queen and knave to put you in.

```
              ♠ K Q 6
              ♡ 9 4 3
              ◇ 9 2
              ♣ A Q 10 8 5
♠ J 7 4                        S      N
♡ Q J 10 8 6    N              2 NT   4 NT
◇ K 7 3       W   E            6 NT   —
♣ 9 6            S
```

You lead the queen of hearts, your partner plays the two and declarer's ace wins. South plays king, knave and a third round of clubs. How do you plan your defence?

Have you counted the declarer's tricks? On the bidding he must have the ace of spades, the king of hearts and ace and queen of diamonds, and it is obvious what is coming. You will be squeezed on the run of the black suits and then thrown in with your last heart to lead away from the king of diamonds. Is there anything you can do about it? Not if declarer reads your discards correctly. All you can do is discard in such a way as to give declarer a chance to go wrong. Your discards on the clubs should be the three and seven of diamonds and then the four of spades. When declarer plays a heart to the king you will play the six, and on the third round of spades you will throw the ten of hearts, concealing the eight. If South believes that you started with four hearts and four diamonds he will now play a heart and go one down.

```
              N              ♠ 10 9 5 2
           W     E           ♡ 7 2
              S              ◇ J 10 8 5
                             ♣ 7 4 2
              ♠ A 8 3
              ♡ A K 5
              ◇ A Q 6 4
              ♣ K J 3
```

Strip-squeezes of this type are by no means uncommon and deceptive discarding is often the defenders' only resource. It is usually safe enough to unguard your honours provided that the key discards are made at an early stage and without signs of distress.

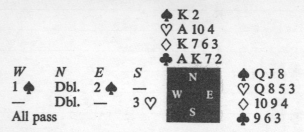

♠ K 2
♡ A 10 4
◇ K 7 6 3
♣ A K 7 2

W	N	E	S
1 ♠	Dbl.	2 ♠	—
—	Dbl.	—	3 ♡
All pass			

♠ Q J 8
♡ Q 8 5 3
◇ 10 9 4
♣ 9 6 3

West leads the ace and another spade against South's three heart contract. A diamond is led from dummy to declarer's queen and West's ace and the diamond return won by the king. Declarer now ruffs a diamond in hand, ruffs a spade on the table and leads dummy's last diamond. How do you play to this trick?

The declarer has made four tricks and the ruff of this diamond will give him five. If he has the king of hearts he will obviously make his contract, so you must assume partner to have that card. What will happen if you discard a club on this trick? South's next move will very likely be to play off ace, king and another club. You will have to ruff the third club and lead a trump, which will allow declarer to make nine tricks if his trumps are headed by the knave. You must therefore play a small trump on dummy's last diamond even though you know declarer will over-ruff. That may enable partner to win the third round of clubs, and the trump lead will come from the right side of the table.

♠ A 9 7 3
♡ K 6
◇ A J 8 5
♣ Q J 8

♠ 10 6 5 4
♡ J 9 7 2
◇ Q 2
♣ 10 5 4

When declarer is playing a cross-ruff a long trump holding is a doubtful asset to a defender. In such circumstances you should normally welcome an opportunity to shorten your trumps.

♠ A 7 5
♡ Q 10 3 2
◇ A Q 7 4
♣ 9 8

♠ 10 8 6 3 2
♡ A 7
◇ K J 6
♣ 6 4 3

N-S game

N	E	S	W
1 NT	2 ♣	3 ♠	—
4 ♠	All pass		

East's two-club bid is the Astro convention showing a distributional hand with hearts and a lower ranking suit. In this case, obviously, it must be a fairly weak distributional hand, so you refrain from doubling and lead the ace of hearts. Partner encourages with the nine and you continue hearts, partner capturing dummy's ten with the knave. East now switches to the knave of clubs. Declarer wins with the queen and leads the two of diamonds. How do you plan the defence?

Declarer must have all the outstanding spades and the ace of clubs, so he can make four spades, two tricks in each minor, and probably a club ruff. If he also makes his fifth spade he will be home, so you must take care not to be thrown in to lead from your vulnerable trump holding. You must play the knave of diamonds on this trick. Now let us say declarer wins with the queen, cashes the ace of spades, leads a club to his ace and ruffs a club, then leads a heart and trumps with the knave. Careful, now! You must on no account throw a diamond on this trick. Declarer has reduced to one trump fewer than you and the only way to keep trump parity is to under-ruff. On a further diamond lead you will play the king and eventually, if partner has that vital ten of diamonds, the defence will make a diamond and a trump trick.

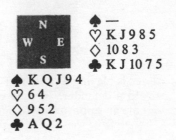

♠ —
♡ K J 9 8 5
◇ 10 8 3
♣ K J 10 7 5

♠ K Q J 9 4
♡ 6 4
◇ 9 5 2
♣ A Q 2

♠ K J 5
♡ Q
◇ J 10 7 6 3
♣ A J 6 2

♠ 10 9 7 4
♡ 5
◇ Q 9 5 2
♣ K Q 9 4

S	N
2 ♡	3 NT
6 ♡	—

You lead the king of clubs against South's six heart contract. The two is played from dummy, your partner plays the three and declarer the five. How do you continue?

Which suit is likely to yield the setting trick? Obviously not clubs. What about spades or diamonds? Declarer will not be missing two aces on this bidding, and if he has a loser in either spades or diamonds it will be discarded on dummy's third round club winner (declarer would not have ducked the first trick if he had three clubs; nor would your partner have played the three from a doubleton). It would appear that the only hope for the defence is that East has a trump trick. He could have J 10 x x, in which case the contract is sure to be defeated. Suppose partner has J x x x. Could declarer make his contract in that case? Only if he can reduce his trumps to the same number as East's and lead through from dummy at the end. He would need four entries to dummy to accomplish that. You can see four potential entries—one club, one heart and two spades. The only one of those entries that you force declarer to use prematurely is the queen of hearts, so you must lead your trump at trick two.

♠ 8 3 2
♡ J 8 6 3
◇ K 8 4
♣ 8 7 3

♠ A Q 6
♡ A K 10 9 7 4 2
◇ A
♣ 10 5

Any other lead allows declarer to make his contract.

♠ 962
♡ 10 9 3
◇ A Q 5
♣ A Q 5 2

S	N		♠ Q J 10 8
1 ♠	2 NT		♡ J 4
4 ♣	—		◇ J 9 7 2
			♣ K 10 6

Your partner leads the five of hearts and your knave is taken by declarer's king. South cashes the ace of spades and blinks when your partner discards the two of hearts. Next comes the seven of clubs, West plays the nine and dummy's queen is finessed to your king. How do you continue?

This has become a double dummy problem, for by now you have a complete blueprint of the distribution and honour strength of the other two hands. Your partner's discards have told you that he started with five hearts to the queen and four clubs. His four diamonds must include the king, otherwise declarer would have tried to eliminate diamonds and hearts from your hand and throw you in for an overtrick. Declarer has four trump tricks, two hearts, two diamonds and a club. His only chance of a tenth trick is to try to make three of the small trumps in his hand by ruffing. Once you realize this the correct defence is easy to find. You must take out one of dummy's entries prematurely by leading a diamond.

♠ —
♡ Q 8 7 5 2
◇ K 10 6 4
♣ J 9 8 3

♠ A K 7 5 4 3
♡ A K 6
◇ 8 3
♣ 7 4

On any other return South will make his contract by *coup en passant*. The contract of three no trumps is, of course, unbeatable as the cards lie.

11 • In the Squeeze Zone

In this chapter I have to assume a higher level of technique in the reader, for in order to defend successfully against squeeze play it is necessary to know what makes a squeeze tick. To the student the subject is full of interest, but it is by no means vital, and any reader who does not wish to be bothered with squeeze defence can omit this chapter without serious detriment to his game.

The squeeze, after all, is only the icing on the cake of good play. Tournaments and matches at any level are not lost through failure to recognize abstruse squeeze positions. They are lost by human lapses in the many simpler situations. If you concentrate on learning how to cut down your errors it will be of much greater benefit to your game than a mastery of all the intricacies of squeeze play.

In theory it is perfectly possible for a player who knows nothing whatever of squeeze play to win national, or even international honours. That this does not happen in practice is because those players who have learned to cut down their errors by accurate card-reading and thus reach the top are the very ones who are sufficiently interested in the game to make an intensive study of squeeze technique.

Like every other phase of defence, squeeze defence is based upon—you've guessed it—counting. It is humiliating to be treated like a wet sponge by the declarer. Sometimes you will be unable to avoid this indignity, but in order to make the most of your opportunities you must keep a careful count of declarer's tricks and make use of all available inferences. Your task is not made lighter by the fact that squeeze defence must usually be inaugurated at an early stage in the play.

There are several different ways in which you may be able to upset the declarer's plans. You will quite often be in a position to attack a vital entry card without which the squeeze cannot function. Sometimes you will be able to control the declarer's loser count and thus disrupt the timing of his squeeze. In certain squeezes the order in which declarer's winners are played off is important, and can be upset. On other occasions you may be able to obliterate menace cards, or invalidate them by sharing the burden of guarding a particular suit with your partner. Finally, there will be times when your only hope will lie in deceptive discarding.

Since the most fruitful field of effort for the defenders is the attack upon entries, we shall start with that. In the problems that follow you must assume that the declarer is a competent squeeze player. Otherwise, in some cases, your defence might be different.

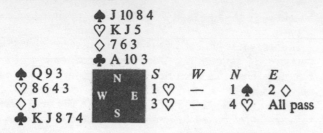

♠ J 10 8 4
♡ K J 5
◇ 7 6 3
♣ A 10 3

♠ Q 9 3
♡ 8 6 4 3
◇ J
♣ K J 8 7 4

	S	W	N	E
	1 ♡	—	1 ♠	2 ◇
	3 ♡	—	4 ♡	All pass

You lead the singleton knave of diamonds against South's four heart contract. East wins with the king, cashes the ace and continues with a middle diamond. After ruffing South's queen what do you lead?

What can the declarer have for his jump rebid? Surely all six trumps plus the ace and king of spades. That means that he has nine winners out of the remaining ten tricks. The count is right for a squeeze and, looking at your honours in the black suits, you can see that you will in fact be squeezed if the declarer has the queen of clubs. If he has ace king bare in spades and queen and another club there is nothing you can do about it. Ten tricks will inevitably fall into declarer's lap. But should he have three spades and the queen of clubs single you can break up the impending squeeze at once by leading your king of clubs.

♠ 7 5 2
♡ —
◇ A K 10 9 8 2
♣ 9 6 5 2

♠ A K 6
♡ A Q 10 9 7 2
◇ Q 5 4
♣ Q

One of the requirements of the simple squeeze, indeed of every type of squeeze, is that there must be an entry in the hand opposite the final squeeze-card. When you can recognize and attack this entry in time the squeeze will disintegrate.

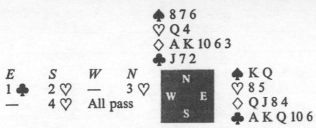

```
                    ♠ 8 7 6
                    ♡ Q 4
                    ◇ A K 10 6 3
                    ♣ J 7 2
E    S    W    N                      ♠ K Q
1♣   2♡   —    3♡         N          ♡ 8 5
—    4♡   All pass    W       E      ◇ Q J 8 4
                         S          ♣ A K Q 10 6
```

Your partner leads the nine of clubs and declarer follows to three rounds, West discarding the two of spades. What do you lead now?

On the bidding the declarer must have six good hearts and the ace of spades. The ace and king of diamonds bring his tally up to nine tricks, and if he has the knave of spades as well you are in imminent danger of being squeezed in spades and diamonds. The obvious lead of a spade cannot be right in that case, because it attacks the wrong entry. It is the entry opposite the squeeze-card that you must attack. There is no certainty of success, but if declarer has a singleton diamond the lead of the diamond queen will cause the squeeze to evaporate.

```
♠ 9 5 4 3 2              N
♡ 7 6 3              W       E
◇ 9 7 5                 S
♣ 9 4
                    ♠ A J 10
                    ♡ A K J 10 9 2
                    ◇ 2
                    ♣ 8 5 3
```

There is a further point of interest in this hand. After your diamond lead if the declarer cunningly leaves his second diamond winner in dummy and runs all his hearts you would probably assume he had a second diamond and abandon spades, trusting your partner to have the knave. West can, and should, prevent you from going wrong like this by discarding all his diamonds at the earliest opportunity.

```
              ♠ Q 8 2
              ♡ A K 7
              ◇ A 10 5 3
              ♣ 8 6 5
♠ K 7 4      ┌─────┐      N      E      S      W
♡ 8 5 2      │  N  │      1 NT   —      3♠     —
◇ 8 6 4      │W   E│      4◇     Dbl.   5♣     —
♣ J 10 9 3   │  S  │      5♡     —      6♠     All pass
             └─────┘
```

In response to your partner's double you lead the six of diamonds against South's slam. The ace is played from dummy, your partner contributing the knave and declarer the two. The queen of spades is run from dummy and you allow it to win. On the two of spades partner throws the king of diamonds, South plays the nine of spades and your king wins. What now?

Your partner's diamond discard might be construed as a Lavinthal showing the queen of hearts, or perhaps he has played low-high with his honour cards to show an odd number of cards and give you a count. At all events, if declarer has a loser in diamonds he will be unable to get rid of it. And if he is void in diamonds with the three top clubs and three hearts headed by the knave, ten or nine, a diamond lead from you will be dangerous. South will ruff, draw your last trump and cash his club tops. On the lead of his second last trump the seven of hearts will be thrown from dummy and your partner will be caught in a ruffing squeeze, unable to keep three hearts and two diamonds. The ruffing squeeze requires two entries in dummy, one to establish the ruffing menace and the other to cash it. You can kill the squeeze by leading a heart.

```
             ┌─────┐      ♠ 5
             │  N  │      ♡ Q 10 6 3
             │W   E│      ◇ K Q J 9 7
             │  S  │      ♣ 7 4 2
             └─────┘
      ♠ A J 10 9 6 3
      ♡ J 9 4
      ◇ 2
      ♣ A K Q
```

```
            ♠ 10 6
            ♡ A K Q 9
            ◇ K 7 5
            ♣ Q 9 8 3
♠ K J 8 4                          N        S
♡ 8 7 5 2      N                   1 ♣      1 ◇
◇ 9 3       W     E                1 ♡      2 NT
♣ J 10 4       S                   3 NT     —
```

You lead the four of spades and your partner wins with the ace. The two of spades comes back and you capture South's queen with your king. How do you continue?

It is gratifying to find that you can make four spade tricks, but where is the setting trick to come from? If East has a minor suit ace you have nothing to worry about, but if he has no ace the situation is not so hopeful. Your partner will then have to have the king of clubs and a diamond stopper. Declarer is quite likely to have the queen of diamonds, which gives him eight top tricks. If you cash your spade tricks now that will rectify the count for the declarer and your partner will be squeezed in clubs and diamonds. You must therefore upset the timing of the threatening squeeze by switching to the knave of clubs at trick three.

```
              N              ♠ A 9 5 2
          W       E          ♡ J 4
              S              ◇ J 10 6 2
                             ♣ K 7 5
            ♠ Q 7 3
            ♡ 10 6 3
            ◇ A Q 8 4
            ♣ A 6 2
```

Note that it would not be good enough to cash a third spade before switching to the knave of clubs, for if South played low from dummy your partner would then be subjected to a strip-squeeze. The run of hearts would force him to discard his remaining spade and his small club. The inference that he was protecting a diamond stopper would be obvious, and South would discard a diamond on the fourth heart and lead a small club from dummy.

```
                    ♠ A K J 5
                    ♡ 10 9 7 2
                    ◇ J 4 3
                    ♣ 9 6
    N-S game                        ♠ Q 8 4
  E    S    W    N           N      ♡ K J
1 NT  Dbl.  2♡  2 NT                ◇ Q 10 9 7 2
 —    3♣    —   3♠       W       E  ♣ A 8 5
 —    6♣   All pass          S
```

Your partner leads the six of diamonds against South's contract of six clubs. The three is played from dummy and your nine
is taken by declarer's king. The king of clubs is now played, and
when you duck declarer continues with the queen, on which your
partner throws the four of hearts. How do you plan your defence?

Declarer has six club tricks and four tricks in diamonds and
spades. Do you think your partner may have the ace of hearts?
Not a chance. On the bidding and the play so far the declarer is
marked with that card, which brings his total up to eleven tricks.
If he also has the queen of hearts the position is hopeless, but your
partner could have the queen. You cannot be sure whether declarer has two or three diamonds, but if he has three nothing is
more certain than that you are going to be squeezed in spades and
diamonds. If he has only two diamonds you can avoid the squeeze
by returning a diamond after winning your ace of clubs.

Any other return is dangerous, for if declarer should happen
to have three spades to the ten you would find yourself under
pressure from a criss-cross squeeze.

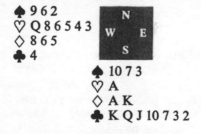

```
      ♠ 9 6 2              N
      ♡ Q 8 6 5 4 3    W       E
      ◇ 8 6 5              S
      ♣ 4
                    ♠ 10 7 3
                    ♡ A
                    ◇ A K
                    ♣ K Q J 10 7 3 2
```

There was a hand in the last chapter where the defender's only hope of defeating a strip-squeeze lay in deceptive discarding. The same tactics have to be employed in a great many other squeeze situations. Whenever the squeeze appears to be inevitable you should look for some means of causing declarer to miscount.

It often happens that declarer is unable to obtain a complete count and, even after the final squeeze-card has been led, there is some ambiguity in the position. On such occasions a little purposeful false-carding may induce the declarer to take the wrong turning when he reaches the crossroads. This applies particularly to those squeezes where for technical reasons the declarer has had to retain the top cards in more than one suit, or more than one top card in a vital suit. This group includes the strip-squeezes, ruffing and criss-cross squeezes, and the more rigid types of double and compound squeezes.

Suppose, in the last hand, that instead of finding the inspired diamond lead your partner had led a heart. You would then be unable to break up the entries for the criss-cross squeeze, and your only defence would lie in trying to persuade the declarer that you started with four cards in both spades and diamonds. On the clubs you might discard first the two of diamonds, then the four of spades and finally the nine of diamonds. When declarer played off one of his diamond winners you would play the ten, the spade king would draw your eight and then, if your partner has played his part and reduced to one card in each suit, the declarer might well go astray and cash his last two high cards in the wrong order.

Of course, if South knows that you will try to fool him in such situations you must try the occasional double bluff by discarding as a beginner would.

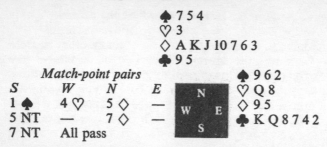

```
                    ♠ 7 5 4
                    ♡ 3
                    ◇ A K J 10 7 6 3
                    ♣ 9 5
     Match-point pairs                    ♠ 9 6 2
 S       W      N      E                  ♡ Q 8
 1♠      4♡     5◇     —                  ◇ 9 5
 5 NT    —      7◇     —                  ♣ K Q 8 7 4 2
 7 NT    All pass
```

After the above lively bidding West leads the knave of clubs against the grand slam. The five is played from dummy, you put in the eight and the ace wins. Declarer cashes the ace of hearts, ace and king of spades and leads a diamond, on which partner discards a heart. How do you plan your defence?

Declarer clearly has the queen of spades; without it he could not conceivably play like this, but he bid spades and must have four of them. That adds up to thirteen tricks on top, four spades, seven diamonds and two aces, and no squeeze is needed. Then what, you may ask, is the hand doing here?

The point is that although *you* can see thirteen tricks on top the declarer cannot, for he does not know the spades are going to break. You must try to persuade him to take a losing spade finesse to your partner's knave by pretending to be squeezed in spades and clubs. Groans and grimaces are barred, unfortunately, so you must rely on your discards alone, coming down to the seven of clubs and the nine of spades as your last two cards. There is no risk in throwing your high clubs even if declarer has the ten. He knows you have the king and queen and if they do not both appear he will certainly throw his club ten and play for the drop in spades.

```
 ♠ J 8 3
 ♡ K J 10 9 7 5 4 2
 ◇ —
 ♣ J 10
                ♠ A K Q 10
                ♡ A 6
                ◇ Q 8 4 2
                ♣ A 6 3
```

♠ Q 8 5 2
♡ 9 6 5 4
◇ K 10
♣ J 10 7

♠ J 10 9 3
♡ Q 10 2
◇ A Q 8
♣ A Q 8

S	W	N	E
1 ♡	1 NT	2 ♡	—
4 ♡	All pass		

You lead the knave of spades against South's four heart contract, your partner following with the four and declarer winning with the ace. Now comes ace, king and another heart, on which your partner throws two small diamonds and a small club. On winning with your queen what do you lead?

A spade lead would give away a trick if declarer has king and another left, so the obvious thing to do appears to be to play ace and another diamond and wait for your club tricks. A closer analysis, however, will convince you that you would wait in vain. The king of diamonds is South's ninth trick and if he has king and another club, as seems likely, the run of the hearts will subject you to a strip-squeeze. In order to protect spades you will be forced to bare your ace of clubs, whereupon the declarer will establish his king.

Is there any way out? Only if you play your partner for the knave of diamonds and lead the diamond queen at trick five. By refraining from cashing the diamond ace you upset the timing of the strip-squeeze. The fact that declarer still has three losers allows room in your hand for an idle card (the ace of diamonds) which can be discarded on the last trump. If declarer attempts to rectify the count by playing a second diamond, your partner will come in with his knave to lead a club through.

♠ 64
♡ —
◇ J 9 7 5 4 2
♣ 9 6 5 4 3

♠ A K 7
♡ A K J 8 7 3
◇ 6 3
♣ K 2

♠ K J
♡ A K 9 5
◇ Q 3
♣ A K J 8 3

N	S			♠ A 2
1 ♣	1 ♠			♡ Q 10 6
2 ♡	3 NT	W	E	◇ 8 6 5
6 NT	—			♣ Q 10 7 5 4

Your partner leads the knave of diamonds against South's contract of six no trumps. The queen wins, and the king of spades is led from dummy. How do you defend?

On this bidding South will not have more than five spades. The first idea that springs to mind is that if your partner's spades are as good as nine high you can block the suit by winning the first spade and returning a diamond. But partner's spades may not be as good as that so you had better have a look at the squeeze possibilities. With four spades, three diamonds, two hearts and two clubs South has a total of eleven tricks. If he has the knave of hearts as well you are in danger of being squeezed in hearts and clubs. To execute this squeeze, however, the declarer would first have to employ the Vienna Coup by playing off the ace and king of the suit in which he holds a trebleton. You can prevent him from doing this and defeat the contract for certain by winning the *second* round of spades and exiting with a diamond.

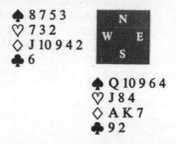

♠ 8 7 5 3
♡ 7 3 2
◇ J 10 9 4 2
♣ 6

♠ Q 10 9 6 4
♡ J 8 4
◇ A K 7
♣ 9 2

Opportunities for defensive tactics of this kind—preventing declarer from unblocking by cutting communications—occur in squeeze play more often than is generally supposed.

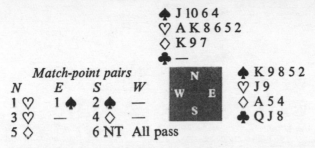

♠ J 10 6 4
♡ A K 8 6 5 2
◇ K 9 7
♣ —

Match-point pairs

N	E	S	W
1♡	1♠	2♣	—
3♡	—	4◇	—
5◇		6 NT	All pass

♠ K 9 8 5 2
♡ J 9
◇ A 5 4
♣ Q J 8

West leads the seven of spades and the knave is played from dummy. You play low, of course, and South has to win with the queen. The queen of diamonds is led and you allow it to win. On a further diamond lead your partner discards the two of clubs and dummy's king is played. How do you plan your defence?

Declarer has five diamond tricks, two spades, two hearts and presumably two top clubs. There can be no spade-club squeeze for lack of entries, and it may appear that South has no play for a twelfth trick. The danger is easy to overlook. If declarer has the tens of hearts and clubs you are likely to find yourself in the grip of a guard squeeze, unable to give partner the protection he needs against a heart finesse. Before the guard squeeze will function, however, South will have to play off one of dummy's heart honours and unblock his ten. Once you realize that the solution to the problem is simple. The squeeze is different but the defence is the same as in the last hand. By holding up until the third round of diamonds and exiting with a spade you can make South sorry he tried for a top.

♠ 7 3
♡ Q 4 3
◇ 2
♣ 9 7 6 5 4 3 2

♠ A Q
♡ 10 7
◇ Q J 10 8 6 3
♣ A K 10

If declarer cashes a heart before leading the third round of diamonds you will kill the squeeze by playing a second heart.

    ♠ A 10 6 2
    ♡ J
    ◇ A K Q 7 6
    ♣ Q J 3

♠ J 9 8 4   *Match-point pairs*
♡ 7 6 3
◇ J 10 5   N   S
♣ K 8 5   1 ◇   2 ♣
                   2 ♠   3 NT
                   —

Not liking your hearts you lead the knave of diamonds, regretting it when you see dummy. On the ace your partner plays the four and the declarer the two. Dummy's queen of clubs is won by East's ace, and he switches to the queen of hearts which is taken by South's ace. Clubs are continued, your king being forced out on the third round while your partner discards the two of hearts. What do you lead now?

On the bidding the declarer is likely to have the king of spades. If your partner has the queen of spades and a diamond stopper he is in danger of being squeezed on the run of the clubs. He will have to let go his spade guard and declarer will make eleven tricks by finessing against your knave. The only way to break up the position and give yourself a chance of regaining parity with those who led a heart originally is to lead a heart now. This will remove an idle card from dummy and the guard squeeze will not work.

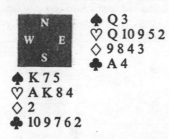

                 ♠ Q 3
                 ♡ Q 10 9 5 2
                 ◇ 9 8 4 3
                 ♣ A 4

♠ K 7 5
♡ A K 8 4
◇ 2
♣ 10 9 7 6 2

One of the requirements of the guard squeeze is that the menace in the same hand as the squeeze-card must, *at the time when the squeeze-card is played*, be accompanied by a winner. Defenders should look out for opportunities of forcing the declarer to play this winner prematurely, thus disrupting the timing of the squeeze.

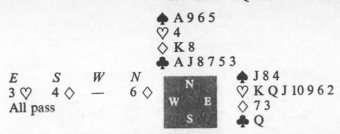

♠ A 9 6 5
♡ 4
♢ K 8
♣ A J 8 7 5 3

E	S	W	N
3 ♡	4 ♢	—	6 ♢
All pass			

♠ J 8 4
♡ K Q J 10 9 6 2
♢ 7 3
♣ Q

West leads a small trump and dummy's eight wins the trick. Declarer plays the ace of clubs and ruffs a club, ace of hearts and ruffs a heart while your partner throws the three of spades, then leads another club from dummy. How do you plan your defence?

You know that declarer started with four hearts and a singleton club but you cannot be sure how many trumps he has. Oddly enough, if he has seven trumps you probably have nothing to worry about. The dangerous situation is where declarer started with six trumps and king and another spade. Then he would have eleven tricks and all the requirements for a double squeeze—except that he has two losers. But he may be planning to rectify his loser count by ducking this trick to your partner, and you can see all too clearly that partner will be able to do nothing to break up the squeeze, for the double menace in spades is not vulnerable to attack. Declarer dare not duck a trick to *you*, however, for you have hearts to cash, so you must play your remaining trump on this trick.

♠ Q 10 7 3
♡ 7
♢ 6 4 2
♣ K 10 9 6 2

♠ K 2
♡ A 8 5 3
♢ A Q J 10 9 5
♣ 4

Declarer has no further chance to duck a trick and, with its timing upset, the squeeze fails to function.

```
                    ♠ J 6 3
                    ♡ A J 5 4
                    ◇ A 9 8 2
                    ♣ 7 6
   ♠ 9 4                          S    W    N    E
   ♡ K 10 9 7           N         2 ♠   —   3 ♠   —
   ◇ 10 5           W       E     4 ♣   —   4 ◇   Dbl.
   ♣ K 9 8 4 2          S         4 ♠   —   5 ♡   —
                                  6 ♠  All pass
```

Since your ten of diamonds might be too useful a card to waste, you lead the five against South's spade slam. On dummy's ace your partner plays the seven and South the four. A spade to the ace is followed by a spade back to the knave, your partner discarding the three of diamonds on the second round. Now comes a small heart from dummy on which East plays the eight, South the queen and you the king. How do you continue?

On this line of play there can be no doubt that declarer started with three hearts, and your partner's eight confirms this view. There are therefore only two unknown cards in South's hand, and it is fairly certain that they are both clubs. If he has ace and queen of clubs you can do nothing but await the inevitable club-heart squeeze. But what if your partner has the club queen? Then declarer will have a double squeeze with clubs as the double menace. It is one of the rigid positional types, inverted in that the double menace is in the same hand as the squeeze-card, but you can see that it will work because the entry to dummy is in the right suit. Say you lead the ten of hearts. Declarer will ruff out your diamond and run the trumps. The last trump will squeeze you out of your club guard, whereupon the heart menace will be thrown from dummy and a heart to the ace will squeeze your partner in clubs and diamonds.

The only way to break up this squeeze is to attack the double menace by leading a club. But if declarer has the knave it will not be good enough to lead a small club, for you will still be squeezed in hearts and clubs. You must lead the king of clubs, for your partner can never be squeezed in clubs and diamonds once the club entry has gone.

♠ 7
♡ 8 2
◊ K Q J 7 6 3
♣ Q 10 5 3

♠ A K Q 10 8 5 2
♡ Q 6 3
◊ 4
♣ A J

The contract can be made by an unusual type of strip-squeeze. If declarer takes the heart finesse, ruffs a diamond and runs the trumps the end position will be as follows:

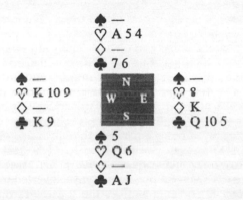

♠ —
♡ A 5 4
◊ —
♣ 7 6

♠ —
♡ K 10 9
◊ —
♣ K 9

♠ —
♡ 8
◊ K
♣ Q 10 5

♠ 5
♡ Q 6
◊ —
♣ A J

On the lead of the last trump no action by West can prevent South from making four of the last five tricks. But that is for the double dummy boys. There is no doubt that the declarer chose the best practical line in playing as he did.

Very often an attack on the double menace is the right action when the defenders see a double squeeze looming ahead. This is especially so when the squeeze is of the automatic type, in which the double menace has to be accompanied by two winners.

Automatic squeezes, as the name implies, are relatively easy to play. The three card double menace creates space for an extra idle card in the opposite hand and gives a greater flexibility to the squeeze. An attack on the double menace converts the squeeze to the more restricted positional type. If it does not kill the squeeze stone dead it is likely to make the declarer's task much harder.

♠ Q 6 3
♥ K J 5 4
◇ A Q 9 6
♣ J 2

S	N		♠ 7 5 4
2 NT	3 ♣		♥ A 2
3 ♠	6 NT		◇ J 10 8 3
—			♣ Q 10 8 4

West leads the ten of spades against South's six no trump contract and South's knave wins the trick. A heart is led to the knave and you win with the ace. What do you lead now?

For his opening bid South must have every outstanding face card, which makes it easy to count his tricks. Four spades, two hearts, three diamonds and two clubs add up to eleven, and you can see that if declarer has the nine of clubs you will inevitably be squeezed in clubs and diamonds. Partner will need to have the club nine and must have a heart stopper. But in that case declarer has a double squeeze in hand with clubs as the double menace. It is the inverted automatic type which will practically play itself. All declarer need do is cash his four spades, discarding a club from dummy. Then the play of the red suits in either order will squeeze both you and your partner out of your club stoppers.

The only hope for the defence is to convert the automatic squeeze to a positional one by attacking the double menace. The lead of the eight of clubs looks risky but it can give the declarer nothing that is not his for the taking anyway.

♠ 10 9 8
♥ 10 8 7 3
◇ 7 4 2
♣ 9 5 3

♠ A K J 2
♥ Q 9 6
◇ K 5
♣ A K 7 6

In fact, with so many chances for his contract, it is highly unlikely that the declarer will risk running your club lead to dummy's knave. He will win with the ace or king and the hand will immediately become full of ambiguity for him. The effect of the club lead is to remove an idle card from dummy and make it impossible for declarer to run the spades without squeezing dummy. Declarer can now get home only if he plays his cards in precisely the right order. The inverted double positional squeeze requires that all winners in the suit menacing the right-hand defender be played off before the squeeze-card (last spade). If declarer plays off the three top diamonds and then runs the spades your partner will be squeezed out of his club guard. The heart menace in dummy can then be thrown on the last spade, and if the last heart trick is won in dummy you will be squeezed in clubs and diamonds.

But it is extremely difficult for declarer to read the position. He has no means of knowing that you control diamonds rather than hearts. When declarer plays the king of diamonds you can try to set him on the wrong road by false-carding with your eight. If declarer now cashes the queen of hearts your partner can give him a further push in the wrong direction by playing *his* eight. After such defence the declarer would need to have a very suspicious mind not to continue with a third round of hearts and thereby ruin his squeeze.

Furthermore, even if he makes the right choice and plays on diamonds he is still not automatically in the clear. After your partner has been squeezed on the lead of the last spade the declarer has another tough decision to make. He has to decide whether hearts are going to break or whether your partner has in fact been squeezed. It would be very easy to go wrong at this point. If the declarer discards anything but the small heart from dummy on the last spade he will go one down in his contract.

♠ 9 7 6
♡ K 10 6 3
◇ K 9 8 4
♣ Q 2

♠ J 5 4 2   ♠ Q 10 3
♡ 8 5 2
◇ Q J 10 6
♣ K 7

S	N
2 ♣	2 NT
6 ♣	—

You lead the queen of diamonds against South's club slam. The king wins in dummy, your partner playing the two and the declarer the three. The queen of clubs is now run to your king. How should you continue?

South must have at least six clubs and he will not be missing an ace. There is not room in his hand for more than three spades so there is no danger of a simple squeeze, and the only double squeeze that might be present is the inverted automatic type with spades as the double menace. It is unnecessary to repeat the argument. By attacking the double menace you can convert the squeeze to a positional one, which you can see will fail because dummy's entry is in the wrong red suit.

♠ Q 10 3
♡ Q J 7 4
◇ 7 5 2
♣ 8 6 4

♠ A K 8
♡ A 9
◇ A 3
♣ A J 10 9 5 3

It is important to realize that there is not the slightest danger in your lead of the two of spades. If declarer's spades are as good as A K 10 he is going to make the contract in any case.

The attack on the double menace can also be an effective defence against positional squeezes when declarer and dummy hold a three-card split menace between them.

```
                    ♠ J 7 6 4
                    ♡ K 7
                    ◇ K 3
                    ♣ A Q 10 6 5
 S    W    N    E                    ♠ 8 5 3
 1◇   1♠   2♣   —                    ♡ Q 10 8 2
 3◇   —    5◇   All pass            ◇ 9 4
                                    ♣ K J 9 3
```

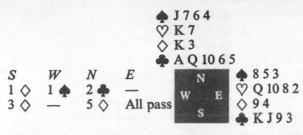

Your partner leads the ace and another trump against South's five diamond contract. The declarer throws dummy's king under the ace, wins the second trump with his ten, and finesses dummy's queen of clubs to your king. How do you plan the defence?

The obvious move is to lead your partner's suit, but a little reflection will convince you that there is no need for haste even if your partner has the ace. Furthermore, South's singleton spade could well be the ace, and if he also has three hearts headed by the ace, there is imminent danger of a double squeeze with hearts as the double menace. The squeeze is a positional one, but the three-card split menace in hearts gives it flexibility and you can see that it will succeed. The solution is beginning to get monotonous. Attacking the double menace removes the flexibility and the ensuing inverted squeeze will fail, as before, because dummy's entry is in the wrong suit. You have to play your partner for the knave of hearts but not necessarily for the nine as well. To avoid the risk of being caught in a simple heart-club squeeze, therefore, you must lead one of your heart honours.

```
          ♠ K Q 10 9 2
          ♡ J 5 4 3
          ◇ A 6
          ♣ 8 2
                              ♠ A
                              ♡ A 9 6
                              ◇ Q J 10 8 7 5 2
                              ♣ 7 4
```

```
              ♠ K 7
              ♡ A K 7 2
              ◇ K J 4
              ♣ Q 8 5 3
   N    S                       ♠ A 2
   1♣   1♠          N           ♡ 9 4 3
   1 NT 3♠      W       E       ◇ Q 10 7 3
   4♠   —           S           ♣ A K J 9
```

Your partner leads the six of clubs, dummy plays low and your knave wins the trick. You continue with the king of clubs on which South drops the ten and West the seven. How do you plan the defence?

On this bidding South is certain to have the ace of diamonds but unlikely to have more than six spades. If his trumps are solid that gives him nine top tricks, and your partner will have to control the third round of hearts. If declarer has three diamonds to the ace and nine you are in danger of being squeezed in diamonds and clubs. Even if West has the diamond nine declarer will have a double squeeze with the three-card split menace in diamonds threatening both defenders. This time, due to the tenace position, you are unable to attack the double menace. Luckily an alternative defence is available. By continuing with your ace of clubs at trick three and a fourth round of clubs when in with the ace of trumps you can rub out the club menace. Should your partner's trumps be as good as ten high this defence will promote a trump trick for him. At all events it will remove any chance of a squeeze.

```
   ♠ 8 5 4
   ♡ Q 10 8 5          N
   ◇ 9 5 2         W       E
   ♣ 7 6 2              S

              ♠ Q J 10 9 6 3
              ♡ J 6
              ◇ A 8 6
              ♣ 10 4
```

Three no trumps would have been a happier contract for North-South as the cards lie.

```
                    ♠ 8 6 4 3
                    ♡ 9 6
                    ◇ A 7 4
                    ♣ A 9 8 2
   ♠ A K Q          N         S        N
   ♡ 10 3                     2 ♡      3 ♣
   ◇ J 6         W      E     4 ♡      5 ◇
   ♣ Q J 7 5 4 3    S         6 ♡      —
```

On your lead of the ace of spades your partner plays the two and declarer the knave. How do you continue?

Unless South is mad that knave must be a singleton and you cannot expect another spade trick. If declarer has seven solid hearts and the minor suit kings (he can hardly have less) he has eleven top tricks. It would be dangerous to continue spades, for declarer might then have enough entries in dummy to isolate the spade menace and squeeze your partner in spades and diamonds. This squeeze can be defeated very easily. There is no need to attack entries. All you have to do is find a safe switch. A heart switch would not necessarily be safe, for dummy's nine could provide the entry needed to ruff out the spades. A diamond lead could give away a trick if partner's diamonds are headed by the queen and nine. What about clubs? Partner cannot be void or he would have doubled for a club lead. Declarer might easily have the king and ten. Well, you have to lead something. What do you choose?

In fact the danger of a diamond lead is illusory. If declarer has K 10 x in diamonds the hand will practically play itself as a double guard squeeze, and you will be unable to protect your partner from the spade-diamond squeeze *and* the diamond finesse. Your proper lead is therefore the knave of diamonds.

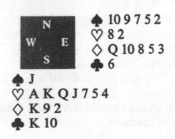

```
                    ♠ 10 9 7 5 2
        N           ♡ 8 2
     W      E       ◇ Q 10 8 5 3
        S           ♣ 6
   ♠ J
   ♡ A K Q J 7 5 4
   ◇ K 9 2
   ♣ K 10
```

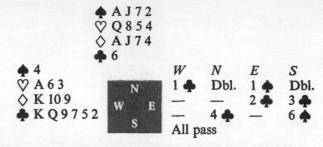

```
              ♠ A J 7 2
              ♡ Q 8 5 4
              ◇ A J 7 4
              ♣ 6
    ♠ 4                        W    N    E    S
    ♡ A 6 3                    1♣   Dbl. 1♠   Dbl.
    ◇ K 10 9                   —    —    2♣   3♣
    ♣ K Q 9 7 5 2              —    4♣   —    6♠
                               All pass
```

You lead the king of clubs against South's six spade contract, your partner playing the four and the declarer the ace. The eight of clubs is led and ruffed in dummy, East completing an echo by playing the three. Dummy's ace of spades is led and a second spade to declarer's king, your partner following while you throw a club. South's queen of diamonds is covered by your king and dummy's ace and your partner plays the three. On the two rounds of trumps that follow your partner and you both discard clubs and a heart is thrown from dummy. Declarer now leads yet another trump. How do you play to this trick?

By this stage you are down to six cards, ♡ A 6 3, ◇ 10 9, ♣ Q, and dummy has ♡ Q 8 5, ◇ J 7 4. To judge from the declarer's play of diamonds he started with queen and another, and his three hearts will surely include the king. It would very likely be fatal for you to discard a heart on this trick, for declarer could then play small to the queen and duck on the way back. A diamond discard will lose if declarer has the eight, so it looks as though your safest course is to part with your club.

Actually it is not so. Declarer still has another trump and you will certainly be forced to part with your diamond stopper on the next round. Since there is no defence unless your partner has the eight of diamonds you may as well let a diamond go immediately. The very fact that you retain your club winner will make it impossible for the declarer to play off his last trump without allowing you to take two tricks as soon as he leads a heart. It is not very often that you can defeat a squeeze by making it too risky for declarer to play off the squeeze card!

♠ 9 3
♡ J 10 9
◇ 8 6 3 2
♣ J 10 4 3

♠ K Q 10 8 6 5
♡ K 7 2
◇ Q 5
♣ A 8

It is usually a mistake for a defender to try to hang on to a stopper that is certain to be forced out sooner or later. If you had retained your diamond stopper at the expense of the queen of clubs, you and your partner would have found yourselves under simultaneous pressure in the same two suits. The ending would have been as shown below.

♠ —
♡ Q 8 5
◇ J 7

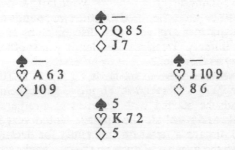

♠ —   ♠ —
♡ A 6 3   ♡ J 10 9
◇ 10 9   ◇ 8 6

♠ 5
♡ K 7 2
◇ 5

This is the type of double automatic strip-squeeze aptly named 'The Vice' by Terence Reese. On the lead of the last spade you would have to part with a diamond, a heart would be thrown from dummy, and your partner would be reluctantly compelled to discard a heart. A diamond to dummy's knave would follow and the lead of the queen of hearts would leave the defenders with one solitary trick.

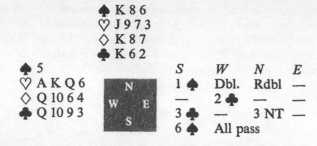

```
              ♠ K 8 6
              ♡ J 9 7 3
              ◇ K 8 7
              ♣ K 6 2
♠ 5                          S      W      N      E
♡ A K Q 6      N             1 ♠    Dbl.   Rdbl   —
◇ Q 10 6 4                   —      2 ♣    —      —
♣ Q 10 9 3   W   E           3 ♣    —      3 NT   —
               S             6 ♠    All pass
```

Your hand is too strong to defend happily against a slam contract and it is with a sense of foreboding that you lead your ace of hearts. Your partner plays the five and declarer the four. That is a pleasant surprise. Declarer will surely not have another heart, and if he has seven spades he will very probably make his contract by a compound squeeze. First a triple squeeze will force you to unguard one of the minor suits, then a double squeeze will take effect with the other minor as the double menace. If you knew which minor suit declarer had a trebleton in you might be able to break up the entries for the squeeze by attacking that suit, playing partner for the knave. But as this is very chancy and the risk of giving away a vital trick too great you decide to continue with a second round of hearts.

Declarer ruffs and reels off four spades. You can spare a card from each suit on these, a heart is thrown from dummy, and partner, after delighting you by following suit three times, also throws a heart on the fourth round of spades. The declarer now leads his final trump. What do you discard on this trick?

The fact that declarer has only six trumps, and therefore only ten winners, gives you renewed hope. If partner has the knave in one of the minor suits you might even defeat the contract by two tricks. But such greedy ideas must be banished. Your job is to defeat the contract by one trick, and to do that all partner need have is the nine of diamonds and the seven of clubs. Your only safe discard is the heart winner. Anything else runs a serious risk of transforming a standard triple squeeze into a progressive squeeze, wherein you will be squeezed again by the winner established by your first discard. The heart discard is safe because when the heart knave is led from dummy the declarer will have to discard ahead of you.

```
            ┌─────────┐      ♠ 9 4 3
            │    N    │      ♡ 10 8 5 2
            │  W   E  │      ◇ 9 3 2
            │    S    │      ♣ 8 5 4
            └─────────┘
      ♠ A Q J 10 7 2
      ♡ 4
      ◇ A J 5
      ♣ A J 7
```

When under pressure in triple or compound squeeze play, defenders will not go wrong if they follow the simple rule of giving up the suit in which the menace lies on their left. Note that your partner also has to select his discards with care in the end position.

```
                 ♡ J
                 ◇ K 8
                 ♣ K 6 2
      ♡ —                     ♡ —
      ◇ Q 10 6                ◇ 9 3 2
      ♣ Q 10 9                ♣ 8 5 4
                 ♡ —
                 ◇ A J 5
                 ♣ A J 7
```

On the last spade a diamond has been thrown from dummy and East has discarded his heart. No matter which king is used to enter dummy, on the knave of hearts East must throw a diamond. By discarding in the suit that dummy abandoned on the previous trick East is, in effect, following the rule of giving up the suit in which the menace lies on his left. Now all West need do is discard in the same suit as South in order to hold him to eleven tricks.

```
              ♠ Q 8 7 2
              ♡ Q 10 3
              ◇ K 4
              ♣ K 10 8 3
♠ A 5 3                        S        N
♡ 8                           2 NT     3 ♣
◇ J 10 9 6 2                   3 ◇      3 ♠
♣ Q J 5 4        N            3 NT     4 ♣
              W     E          4 ♡      4 NT
                 S            6 NT      —
```

You lead the knave of diamonds against South's contract of six no trumps and the trick is won by dummy's king, your partner playing the three and South the five. Two rounds of hearts are won by dummy's queen and declarer's knave. When you discard a diamond on the second round, South plays the four of spades to dummy's queen, East playing the six, and continues with two more rounds of hearts won by his ace and king. You can spare a club on the first of these, but what do you throw on the second?

The declarer must have three spades to play as he has done and his hand is easily counted. Although he has only ten top tricks and therefore three losers, this feels uncommonly like a triple squeeze. You are in fact in the grip of a three suit strip-squeeze, and there is no obvious way of preventing the squeeze from repeating and thus gaining two tricks for the declarer.

The usual rule of giving up the suit in which the menace is held on your left will not help you this time, for dummy has an extended menace in clubs. A club discard would give declarer his two extra tricks straight away. To bare your spade ace is no good either. Declarer would play his small spade to knock out your ace and eventually the play of the spade king would squeeze you again in clubs and diamonds. If you throw a diamond the same fate is in store for you—you will be squeezed again on the lead of South's fourth diamond. Then is there no hope?

So far we have not considered the spade position in detail. If declarer's remaining spades are as good as K 10 there is nothing you can do, but if your partner has the knave and ten you can break up this squeeze for certain by making the unusual discard of the spade ace.

This will give declarer his eleventh trick immediately, but the very fact that you have parted with a winner will upset the timing of the ensuing simple squeeze. Declarer will have no means of rectifying the count, for he cannot duck a spade to your partner without allowing him to make his long heart.

♠ J 10 6
♡ 9 7 6 5 2
♢ 7 3
♣ 9 6 2

♠ K 9 4
♡ A K J 4
♢ A Q 8 5
♣ A 7

Declarer let you off the hook by making that premature spade lead. If he had kept dummy's spade entry intact the lead of the fourth heart would have found you without resource.

12 • The Final Count

The last chapter has turned out to be twice as plump as any other, and I am guiltily aware that the space it occupies is perhaps out of proportion to the importance of the subject. Anyway, after the caviare of squeeze defence it will be quite a relief to get back to the bread and butter of plain counting. I almost wrote pure counting, but of course pure counting in bridge is as much a contradiction in terms as pure mathematics in engineering. It is applied counting that we are concerned with. From the defenders' point of view counting that cannot be applied to the task of bringing about declarer's downfall is nothing but wasted effort.

In this final selection of hands the information gained from counting can be applied with good effect.

♠ J 7 4
♡ 6
◇ K Q J 9 3
♣ A J 9 5

S   N
1 NT¹ 3 ◇
3 NT   —

♠ K 9 8 2
♡ K Q J
◇ 7 6
♣ 8 6 4 3

Against South's contract of three no trumps your partner leads the three of hearts, and declarer drops the four under your knave. How should you continue?

Your partner appears to have led from a five-card suit. If his hearts are headed by the ace and ten you will defeat the contract easily enough, but he could have a heart suit headed by the ten and an outside entry. The only outside entry card that is likely to help the defence is the ace of diamonds. In that case you will have to defend with care. A return of the king of hearts would give away the precise nature of your holding, and the declarer would be quick to take advantage of the blockage by going up with his ace and playing on diamonds. Instead you should play the queen of hearts at trick two. Declarer may now decide to play for you to have the ace of diamonds and hold up his ace until the third round. If you are allowed to hold the third round as well you will have to lead a spade and hope your partner has the queen.

♠ Q 6
♡ 10 8 5 3 2
◇ A 8 4 2
♣ 10 7

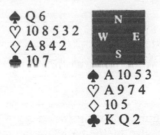

♠ A 10 5 3
♡ A 9 7 4
◇ 10 5
♣ K Q 2

An alternative defence with an equal chance of success would be to play the queen of hearts at trick one and continue with the king.

¹ 12–14 points.

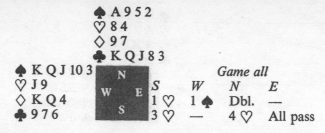

♠ A 9 5 2
♡ 8 4
◇ 9 7
♣ K Q J 8 3

♠ K Q J 10 3
♡ J 9
◇ K Q 4
♣ 9 7 6

Game all

S	W	N	E
1 ♡	1 ♠	Dbl.	—
3 ♡	—	4 ♡	All pass

You lead the king of spades against South's four heart contract. The two is played from dummy, your partner plays the six and declarer the four. How should you continue?

Instinct tells you to knock out that ace of spades before it can be used as an entry for dummy's clubs, but a close examination of the spots is usually a better guide. Declarer cannot have three spades or he would not dare to duck the first trick. Also, with three spades he would probably not have disturbed his partner's double. Could he have a doubleton spade then? Only if your partner has failed to echo to show *his* doubleton. If you trust your partner you are forced to the conclusion that declarer has no more spades. Then why did he duck the first trick? There can be only one answer to that question. Declarer has the singleton ace of clubs. On a further spade lead he intends to discard the blocking ace of clubs and get some diamonds away on dummy's clubs. You can defeat this plan by refusing to continue with a second spade. A trump is your safest lead.

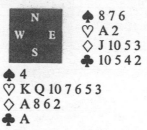

♠ 8 7 6
♡ A 2
◇ J 10 5 3
♣ 10 5 4 2

♠ 4
♡ K Q 10 7 6 5 3
◇ A 8 6 2
♣ A

This hand appears to be a fugitive from Chapter Eight.

♠ Q 10 8 6
♡ A 2
◇ A K J 8 5
♣ Q 7

N	S
1 ◇	2 ♣
2 ♠	3 NT
—	

♠ K J 7 3
♡ 9 8 4
◇ Q 10 6 2
♣ 6 5

Your partner leads the nine of spades against South's three no trump contract. The ten is played from dummy, you cover with the knave and South plays the four. How should you continue?

You cannot count declarer's hand with any certainty at this stage, but you know that he has two spade tricks, one heart and two diamonds. He will need to make several club tricks to make his contract. Have you asked yourself why declarer conceded a tempo by ducking the first trick instead of winning with the ace? It is probably because the ace of spades is his only sure entry card and he does not wish to use it before the clubs are established. What is bad for the declarer must be good for the defence. You should therefore continue with your king of spades to make sure of knocking out South's ace. That will give declarer an extra spade trick, but it may make it impossible for him to win more than one club. He will have to play on diamonds instead, which will suit you fine.

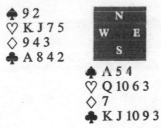

♠ 9 2
♡ K J 7 5
◇ 9 4 3
♣ A 8 4 2

♠ A 5 4
♡ Q 10 6 3
◇ 7
♣ K J 10 9 3

♠ 1082
♡ A K Q 10 7 3
◇ J 9 2
♣ K

N	S
1 ♡	2 ♣
2 ♡	2 NT
3 NT	—

♠ Q 3
♡ 6 5 2
◇ Q 7 4
♣ A J 9 4 2

Your partner leads the four of spades and your queen holds the trick. How do you plan your defence?

Prospects are not very hopeful, for you can see the hearts are breaking. What is the spade position? It is hardly likely that South would hold up with four to the ace. Your partner must have led from ace and king and declarer has four to the knave. To account for his bidding declarer must also have the two top diamonds and the queen of clubs. That gives him eight tricks on top and he can develop a ninth trick in either spades or clubs according to your defence. Is there any way to stop him?

If you reflect for a moment on the fact that dummy has no outside entry and declarer perhaps no more than one heart, the answer may become plain. Declarer's hand will be ruinously squeezed if the hearts are run prematurely, so your proper return at trick two is a heart.

♠ A K 7 4
♡ J 9 8
◇ 10 8 6 3
♣ 7 6

♠ J 9 6 5
♡ 4
◇ A K 5
♣ Q 10 8 5 3

Declarer will probably run five hearts, discarding three clubs and a diamond from his hand, and then lead a spade. Whatever he does, as long as you and your partner read his discards correctly, you can hold him to eight tricks.

♠ 10 8 7
♡ K Q 6
◇ 9 5 4
♣ K 10 7 2

			S	N
♠ K 3			1 ♠	1 NT
♡ J 10 9 5 3 2			2 ◇	2 ♠
◇ 7 2			4 ♣	—
♣ A J 5				

You lead the knave of hearts against South's four spade contract and dummy's queen is captured by East's ace. Your partner returns the eight of hearts, South follows and the king wins the trick. On dummy's ten of spades your partner plays the four and declarer the two. How do you plan your defence?

What is South's distribution likely to be? There is an outside chance that it is 5-2-4-2, but 5-2-5-1 is more probable. It could well be that declarer has no other losers in diamonds or spades, but just in case he requires a further finesse in either suit you must make sure that you are never on lead again. You should take your king of trumps and then cash the club ace before exiting with a heart.

♠ 9 5 4
♡ A 8
◇ Q 8 6
♣ Q 9 6 4 3

♠ A Q J 6 2
♡ 7 4
◇ A K J 10 3
♣ 8

If you failed to cash your ace of clubs at trick four you might be thrown in with it at trick five, at which stage any lead you made would give declarer the entry he requires in dummy to enable him to take the diamond finesse.

♠ A J 10
♡ K 7 6
◇ J 7 6
♣ A 10 8 2

S   *N*
1 NT[1]   3 NT

♠ K 8 6 5
♡ A J 9
◇ K 10 5 2
♣ 7 4

Your partner leads the seven of spades against South's three no trump contract. The ten is played from dummy, you win with the king and South plays the four. You return the five of spades to dummy's knave, South playing the nine and West the three. The six of diamonds is led from dummy and South's queen wins the trick. Declarer cashes the king and queen of clubs and leads a third round, on which your partner plays the knave. What should you discard on the third and fourth rounds of clubs?

South's king and queen of clubs, ace and queen of diamonds and queen of spades add up to thirteen points, so your partner must have the queen of hearts. It is painfully clear what declarer intends to do to you. After the fourth round of clubs he will play a diamond to his ace, a spade back to dummy, and throw you in with the diamond lead away from your ace of hearts. Is there any way of avoiding this fate? Yes, if your partner has four diamonds and hangs on to them. On the ace of clubs you should throw the nine of hearts in an attempt to clarify the position for your partner, and on the fourth club you must throw a spade. When the diamond is led you will play your ten, and when you are eventually thrown in you may be able to cross the table with a small diamond for your partner to lead a heart.

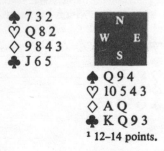

♠ 7 3 2
♡ Q 8 2
◇ 9 8 4 3
♣ J 6 5

♠ Q 9 4
♡ 10 5 4 3
◇ A Q
♣ K Q 9 3

[1] 12–14 points.

♠ A K Q J
♡ K 10 9
◇ Q J 9 6 4
♣ J

♠ 10 9 8 3
♡ Q J 5
◇ K 8 7 2
♣ K 4

N	S
1 ◇	1 NT
2 NT	—

Your opening spade lead turns out to be safe, if not dynamic. A diamond is led to South's ten and you duck. South cashes the ace, your partner following, and crosses in spades to lead the queen of diamonds, on which East discards the seven of clubs. What do you lead after taking your king of diamonds?

It is not difficult to place the cards on this hand. For the bidding to make any sense your partner must have the outstanding aces and declarer the club queen. Then perhaps you should lead the club four to your partner's ace. A club back to your king will give dummy an awkward discard. The trouble is that if a heart is thrown you will be in doubt whether to continue with the queen of hearts or the five. If a winner is thrown from dummy you are no better off. You can put dummy in with a spade or a diamond but at the end declarer will be able to lead a heart equal from dummy and still have a fifty-fifty chance of making his contract.

The better shot is to lead the five of hearts before touching clubs. Now declarer's percentage play will be to go up with the king, for he can see that he will be one down if the nine loses to either the knave or the queen. As happens occasionally, the correct play of the king will result in the cruel fate of two down.

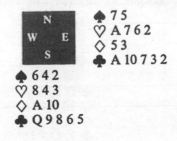

♠ 7 5
♡ A 7 6 2
◇ 5 3
♣ A 10 7 3 2

♠ 6 4 2
♡ 8 4 3
◇ A 10
♣ Q 9 8 6 5

    Your partner leads the two of hearts and your king is taken by South's ace. The knave of spades is led and run to your queen. How should you continue?

    For the defence you can count two spades and probably, if partner has led from the queen, a heart trick. It is not immediately clear where the setting trick can be found. What about declarer's tricks? Since his trumps are so weak in high cards he is likely to have six of them. And if your partner has the queen of hearts declarer must have ace and king of diamonds for his bidding. With the help of the club finesse declarer will therefore make ten tricks unless you can find a quick way to stop him. If South has three clubs there is nothing you can do, but if he has a doubleton you can prevent him enjoying more than two club tricks by taking out his clubs before your trumps are exhausted. You must lead a club at trick three and another club when you win the second round of trumps.

    ♠ 7 5
    ♡ Q 10 4 2
    ◊ 9 5 2
    ♣ Q 10 8 3

    ♠ J 10 9 8 6 3
    ♡ A J
    ◊ A K 7
    ♣ 5 4

    It would be a mistake to give partner his heart trick first. Partner might have difficulty in judging the situation and could well switch to diamonds.

♠ A Q 9 7 6
♡ Q 3
◇ Q 6
♣ J 8 7 2

			S	N
♠ K 8 5 2	**N**		1 ♡	1 ♠
♡ A 5	**W**	**E**	2 ♡	3 ♡
◇ 10 9 7 4			4 ♡	—
♣ A 9 3	**S**			

Your lead of the ten of diamonds is covered by dummy's queen and won by your partner's ace. East returns the two of diamonds and South wins with the king. The four of trumps is now led and you play the five, dummy the queen and East the six. A second trump is played to your ace, East playing the two and South the king. How should you continue?

You are not likely to make a spade trick, so you will need two tricks from clubs. But on the bidding declarer is very likely to have the king of clubs and it would be unwise to open the suit. Would a diamond lead be safe? Presumably the declarer would have ruffed a losing diamond if he had one. It looks as though his diamond holding was K J x. You know from your partner's echo that declarer started with six trumps, and the danger is now becoming apparent. With the spade finesse declarer has nine tricks. If his spades are as good as knave and another he will make his contract, for your partner's spade ten will fall on the second round. Come to think of it, if South has even a small doubleton in spades you are going to be subjected to a strip-squeeze on the run of the trumps and declarer will make ten tricks. The only way to break up this position and force South to lead clubs himself is to lead your king of spades.

♠ 10 4
♡ 7 6 2
◇ A 8 5 2
♣ Q 10 5 4

♠ J 3
♡ K J 10 9 8 4
◇ K J 3
♣ K 6

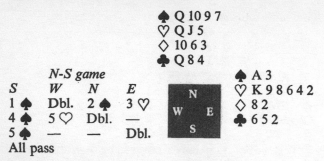

♠ Q 10 9 7
♡ Q J 5
◇ 10 6 3
♣ Q 8 4

N-S game

S	W	N	E
1 ♠	Dbl.	2 ♠	3 ♡
4 ♠	5 ♡	Dbl.	—
5 ♠	—	—	Dbl.

All pass

♠ A 3
♡ K 9 8 6 4 2
◇ 8 2
♣ 6 5 2

After a contentious auction your partner leads the ace of hearts against South's doubled contract of five spades. The declarer ruffs and leads the king of spades, on which your partner discards the seven of hearts. How do you plan your defence?

The obvious thing to do, after winning your trump trick, is to return a diamond up to dummy's weakness, but it might be as well to reflect for a moment on partner's carefully non-committal discard of the heart seven. Surely your partner's diamonds cannot be as good as A Q, or he would have signalled for a lead. For the same reason your partner is unlikely to have the king in one minor and the ace in the other. Just about the only holding that would account for partner's uncertainty is a diamond suit to the queen and knave and clubs to the ace and knave. In that case you can count declarer for six spade tricks, one heart by trump finesse, two diamonds and a club, totalling ten tricks. Is there any way in which he could make an eleventh?

Declarer is unlikely to have a singleton king of clubs, for with six clubs partner would have signalled for you to lead the suit. He might well have a doubleton though, in which case on regaining the lead he could put partner on the spot by leading his small club. If partner takes his ace, the queen of clubs and the heart will furnish discards for two diamonds, while if partner plays low the king of clubs will eventually be discarded on the heart winner and declarer will simply concede a diamond.

Is there anything you can do about it if that is the position? There certainly is. You can upset declarer's timing by forcing him to take his heart trick before he knows what to discard from his hand. After winning your ace of trumps you should lead a small heart.

The full hand is as follows:

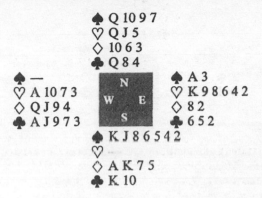

                ♠ Q 10 9 7
                ♡ Q J 5
                ◇ 10 6 3
                ♣ Q 8 4

    ♠ —   ♠ A 3
    ♡ A 10 7 3   ♡ K 9 8 6 4 2
    ◇ Q J 9 4   ◇ 8 2
    ♣ A J 9 7 3   ♣ 6 5 2

                ♠ K J 8 6 5 4 2
                ♡
                ◇ A K 7 5
                ♣ K 10

Any other lead allows South to make his contract by the
avoidance play described.

The last was a difficult hand, but one that well illustrates the
main theme of this book. No reader who has waded through to
this final page is likely to quarrel with my assertion that counting
is the prime ingredient of successful defence. To acknowledge the
truth of this from the security of an armchair is easy enough. To
act on it in the heat of battle around the green baize table is
another matter. Anyone with the ability and the determination to
do so will soon find that he is leaving a trail of unhappy declarers
behind him.